T0191397

TO DO

MIKAEL KROGERUS
ROMAN TSCHÄPPELER

TO DO

41 TOOLS TO START, STICK WITH, AND FINISH THINGS

Translated from the German by Gesche Ipsen

W. W. NORTON & COMPANY

Independent Publishers Since 1923

Author's note: Most of the chapters in this book were first published in a shorter version in Tages-Anzeiger's Das Magazin, *in Zurich. We are grateful to the editor-in-chief, Finn Canonica, for his faith and inspiration.*

First published in Great Britain in 2023 by Profile Books as *The Get Things Done Book: 41 Tools to Start, Stick with and Finish Things*
First published in 2021 in Switzerland by Kein & Aber AG Zurich

For information about special discounts for bulk purchases, please contact W. W. Norton Special Sales at specialsales@wwnorton.com or 800-233-4830

Manufacturing by Versa Press

ISBN 978-1-324-07535-6

W. W. Norton & Company, Inc.
500 Fifth Avenue, New York, N.Y. 10110
www.wwnorton.com

W. W. Norton & Company Ltd.
15 Carlisle Street, London W1D 3BS

1 2 3 4 5 6 7 8 9 0

CONTENTS

YOU MAKE YOUR OWN
PATH AS YOU WALK

Why is it that checking all the boxes, completing a task – in short, getting things done – is so immensely satisfying? Nothing else compares to it. The sense of pride we experience when we've *done* something is one of the best feelings in the world. Whether you've finished doing all the dishes, finally submitted your tax return, given a client presentation or had a frank discussion, and whether you're a first-year intern or a long-standing member of the board: the feeling that you've done something (and done it *well*) spurs you on, makes you itch to get to work on the next thing, and the next one, and the one after that.

However, we don't "get things done" the same way every time. Sometimes we're bursting with energy: we roll up our sleeves and get positively carried away by the task in front of us, particularly when it happens to dovetail with our abilities and our goals. We're in what occupational psychologists call a "state of flow." The question is: how can we achieve this state more often?

At other times we falter, unsure if we're on the right path, even questioning the whole project. Similarly, we can often be lazy, inefficient or timid, and not manage to get anything done at all. The question here is: where can we find the necessary inspiration, encouragement and techniques to help us tackle something afresh, and differently?

We designed this book with both scenarios in mind. It will help you intensify the highs as well as smooth out the lows.

This book is about how to embark on a project, how to get started, stop procrastinating, and give yourself a good kick in the pants now and then. It's also about how to immerse yourself in what you're doing, how to take a breather and start again, how to stick with something and see it through to the end. We've brought together all sorts of techniques, theories and tricks, and tried them out in today's digitized, fragmented and "remote" world of work, to find out how we can reach decisions more quickly, have more fun and improve the outcome of the projects we undertake.

We're not suggesting that you should obsess about growth. We aren't promoting "productivity porn" or preaching a Puritan work ethic. This book isn't about how to make everything more productive and streamlined, but about how to focus on what's important to you, on the things that are actually meaningful and valuable, both for you and for others. Discovering your true passion is one of life's great joys. We all know what it feels like when we've had a great day, and the second we get home we start waxing lyrical about what happened and the part we played in it. We have all seen that unmistakable sparkle in someone's eyes, when they tell you about a venture they're really excited about. This book is like a little road map that shows you how to discover this feeling if you haven't already – and how to foster it, if you already have.

One last thing before we start: the techniques we describe here aren't one-size-fits-all solutions. Choose the ones that appeal to you. Try this and that, pick a technique and build on it or tweak it. Some will suit you, others won't. The only thing we can say for certain is that this book wouldn't exist without this book.

Mikael Krogerus   *Roman Tschäppeler*

Doing things

PROCRASTINATION: HOW TO MAKE A START IN THE FIRST PLACE

Procrastination – from the Latin *pro* ("forward") and *crastinus* ("belonging to tomorrow"), i.e. postponing a task till the next day – is the feeling of paralysis that overcomes us when we know that we ought to be doing one thing but do another instead. Or do nothing at all. Around 80 percent of us are afflicted by this common problem, while the remaining 20 percent are *chronic* procrastinators.

Much research has been done on why we procrastinate, and it has nothing to do with laziness. Rather, it's the result of one part of your brain, the one that wants to be happy *now*, battling with the part that knows we have to get something done first, so that we can be happy *later*. This is the so-called temporal motivation theory, which identifies these four reasons for procrastinating:

1. "Expectancy": we mistakenly believe that we can't cope with the task at hand, which lowers our motivation even to get started.
2. "Sensitivity to delay": we fail to realize the extent to which procrastination prevents us from completing the task on time.
3. "Value": we underestimate the pleasure we'll gain from completing the task on time.
4. "Metacognition": we don't reflect enough on what we are (not) doing. If we reflected more, we would realize right

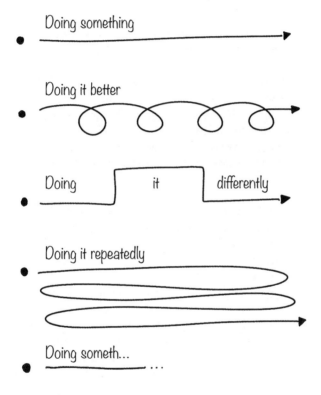

Different ways of (not) doing something.

away that our delaying tactics are merely deceiving and hurting us.

The effects of procrastination have been well documented: problems at work, reduced income, ill health, more stress and more frequent anxiety attacks (because the things we haven't done hang over our heads like the sword of Damocles).

What has been less well researched is how we can *stop* procrastinating. However, some people have come up with potentially useful ideas: for example, Jason Wessel from Brisbane's Griffith University has devised a technique to help those who habitually miss deadlines. He suggests that if you suffer from procrastination, you should ask yourself these questions twice a day:

1. Emotion: how will you feel if you don't complete the task?
2. Vision: what would a productive person do if they were in your shoes?
3. Plan: what is the one thing you can do to achieve your goal on time?
4. Progress: what is the one thing you need to do next?

But be warned: this isn't a magic formula. Nothing will change simply because you spend a minute or two answering these questions. Rather, it's a kind of micro-dosed behavioral therapy: you should regularly take a moment to think about these reflection points. For example, Wessel's weight-loss app (Contemplate) has regular reminders built into it.

There are all sorts of other interesting techniques to help you avoid getting distracted, and to help you get started on whatever it is you need to do (as Wessel drily remarks, *any* technique that helps, helps). We ourselves have found *The Pomodoro Technique* (p. 10) and *The 5-Second Rule* (p. 34) especially useful.

THE POMODORO TECHNIQUE: HOW A TOMATO CAN HELP YOU FOCUS

The Pomodoro technique is one of the best, and simplest, ways to avoid distractions and get started on something – whether it's doing your homework, sorting out your tax return or writing a research proposal. (It's named after a kitchen timer shaped like a tomato.)

1. Turn off your Wi-Fi. Put your smartphone on airplane mode.
2. Set the timer for 25 minutes and work without interruptions until it goes off.
3. Take a short break of a few minutes. (It won't be easy, but try *not* to turn your Wi-Fi back on. Get up for a bit, stretch, take a deep breath or do ten push-ups.)
4. Set the timer for another 25 minutes and stay focused on your work until it goes off again.
5. After three or four rounds, take a longer break. Turn the Wi-Fi back on.

That's it. Really. It sounds like nothing, but we wouldn't have finished this book without it. And Francesco Cirillo, who came up with this technique, would never have completed his degree.

One more thing: the Pomodoro technique won't stop you from producing trash, but it will make you produce *something*. The truth is that you need to do a lot of something in order to do it well, whether it's cooking, writing, composing music or teaching.

Focus on your work for 2 hours:

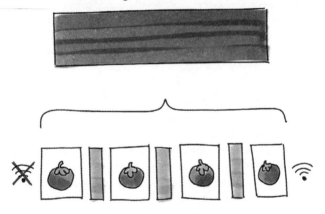

The productivity formula: focus for four sets of 25 minutes, with five-minute breaks.

COMPARTMENTALIZATION: WHY YOUR THOUGHTS NEED A FILING SYSTEM

One of the things that makes our modern working lives particularly tough is that we have so many things on our plate. How to deal with them all? Not just unanswered emails, cost-cutting efforts, short-term projects and long-term strategies, but truly everything: childcare, aging grandparents, the dream of owning a home, our health, hobbies, friendships, love, sleep – all of this is important, so we want to, and need to, deal with all of it. But how?

By compartmentalizing.

Compartmentalization shouldn't be confused with pigeon-holing. It's not about forcibly categorizing things. Rather, it's a mechanism that helps us cope with the multitude of often contradictory impressions and demands on our time. To compartmentalize means to concentrate on one thing as you tune out everything else – opening one drawer and closing all the others.

The entrepreneur Ryan Blair explains compartmentalization this way: picture your life as a house. Everything that's important has its own room. And in each room there's a whiteboard, with a mathematical equation on it that you need to solve. However, in each room there is also a timer. The time you have to solve the equation depends on how complex it is, but the longest you have is 60 minutes. Sometimes you only manage

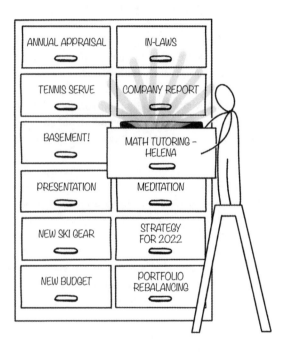

"Compartmentalization" means tackling each task in turn, and never leaving several "open" at once.

to solve it partially, sometimes you solve it completely. Whatever the case, as soon as the timer goes off you should leave the room, close the door behind you and proceed to the next room, and then dedicate yourself to the next task. Open the door, focus, work on the task, stop, close the door – one room after another. And so it goes, for the rest of your life.

We can well imagine that living in a house full of mathematical formulas and a constantly buzzing timer will leave you feeling stressed, rather than motivated. So how about this:

1. First, decide what is important in your life – things you don't want to do without, or can't avoid. Put each of these in a "room." (Even as you just do this part of the exercise – if, that is, you do it properly – you may find yourself spending quite a lot of time in "rooms" that you don't, in all honesty, care very much about. To find out what's really important to you, check out *The 5/25 Rule*, p. 124.)
2. Before you enter a new "room" – whether it's going to an important meeting, heading out for a jog or attending a parent-teacher conference – prepare yourself mentally for this particular room. To stumble into a situation unprepared, only then orientating yourself and focusing on what's going on, is a fatal mistake. Instead, do the opposite: take your time to think each situation through in advance, and ask yourself questions such as: why are we having this meeting? Who will be there? What do they want? What do I want? Sometimes you'll only need a few minutes to get ready, sometimes several hours. And then, once you're in a situation, give it your undivided attention (and don't start thinking about the next one yet). Be present. That's your greatest resource.
3. When you leave the "room," leave the task behind too, i.e.

never carry an issue over from room A to room B. To make sure this doesn't happen, it helps to review the room as you leave it. For example, after a meeting, an exercise session or a parent-teacher conference, briefly note down the important bits. What are your key takeaways?

Compartmentalizing also means coming to terms with the fact that some things won't turn out perfectly. That's the price you have to pay: you will never achieve 100 percent perfection in any room, but you might reach 80 percent in all of them.

RAPID PROTOTYPING: WHY "TRIED" IS BETTER THAN "PERFECT'

"The only way to experience an experience is to experience it," said Bill Moggridge (1943–2012), co-founder of the legendary design consultancy IDEO. What exactly did he mean by that? Well, what he meant was that it's hard to put a new experience – a product, a service, a software solution, whatever it might be – into words. You have to *experience* it before you can know whether you're prepared to spend money on it. This is why he encouraged his designers to produce ideas rather than describe them. A physical object, even if it's just a rough sketch or a clunky model made out of a pizza box, has an astonishing ability to guide our imagination in an unexpected direction.

As the designers discovered, a prototype doesn't have to be high quality. What's much more important is that you can *grasp* its content (or function), and thus get a solid idea of the product or offer in question. "Hold it, use it, talk about it," Moggridge said, as his staff got their hands dirty.

Building a rough model is called "rapid prototyping." According to IDEO, a rapid prototype should have three qualities: it should be **rough**, **rapid** and **right**.

It doesn't need to be perfect; a **rough** model is enough to help us identify the product's essential qualities. If the rocking chair had been developed using rapid prototyping, its designer

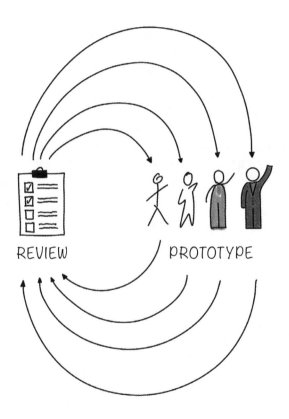

REVIEW PROTOTYPE

Iterative production prototyping: test it, get feedback, improve it.

would have focused only on the "rocking" aspect. They would have ignored other aspects, such as that the chair should also be comfortable and beautiful, have a back and arm rests, and be made of oak – because you can easily picture those qualities by merely looking at an ordinary armchair. What we can't picture, however, is the fact that the new chair rocks.

At the same time, the prototype should be produced **rapidly**, so that you don't need lots of time to tweak it afterward. The idea is that you model the concept quickly and playfully, before you put it to the test and gather feedback – from users, customers and colleagues – which you then either integrate or reject during the next development loop. That way, you can create more than one prototype, stay flexible, and avoid spending a lot of money (and time) on developing something the market doesn't want (see *New Work*, p. 80).

Finally, the prototype should also answer the **right** question. Every product should solve an actual problem (or perhaps create a new need), so the question we should keep asking ourselves during the development stage is: does this answer the original question?

You may ask: "What does this have to do with me?"

When we hear the word "prototype," we usually think of manufactured products such as rockets or cell phones, but this technique also comes in handy if you want to restructure a department, convert a loft or design a new business card. For instance, before deciding whether to proceed with a revamped department, have the new teams work together for a week and then interview the individual team members. If you want to convert a loft, build a model out of a cardboard box; and if you want to redesign your business card, draft three options and send them to ten people. If the feedback turns out wholly negative, celebrate your failure – we learn more from our failures than our triumphs. Every prototype that fails during an early development loop represents one less chance of failure during the final phase.

At heart, rapid prototyping combines two ideas. First, perfection is a bastard. Yes, we all want a solution that's 100 percent perfect, but if you always seek perfection your lofty expectations will stand in your way, and you'll never get anything done. "Good enough" is usually good enough. Better try something out first and improve it along the way, than deliver a supposedly finished product. Better not as good as it might be, than not on the market at all.

Second, don't trust your judgment. Even if you think that your product is brilliant, always ask people who know about such things what they think, especially those who are supposed to eventually buy it. And don't take negative feedback as obliterating critique, but see it as a learning opportunity. Criticism is like exercise: annoying, but good for you. (See *Radical Transparency*, p. 92.)

BURSTY COMMUNICATION: THINGS YOU SHOULD KNOW ABOUT WORKING FROM HOME

The number of people working from home has been on the rise for years. Then Covid came, and the number exploded. Working from home can be cheaper, more comfortable and safer – but is it more effective too?

Even before Covid, some people wondered whether working remotely might be negatively affecting staff loyalty, productivity and openness to innovation. Apple, Meta and Google – firms seen as role models particularly by start-ups, but also by smaller, medium-sized businesses – might depend a lot on remote teams, but even they have started questioning the practice and are trying to tempt employees back to the workplace with free meals and laundry services. The main argument behind this is that casual chats have long been seen as the chief source of new ideas – and when people work from home they don't meet by the coffee machine anymore. (Steve Jobs once even wanted all Apple HQ bathrooms to be installed in the center of the building, so that staff would keep bumping into each other.)

Yet there are times, such as during a pandemic, when we have no choice but to work from home, and a study by Christoph Riedl and Anita Williams Woolley suggests that this doesn't mean you can't continue to have creative exchanges with your colleagues. Their study distinguishes between two types of communication: normal and intensive.

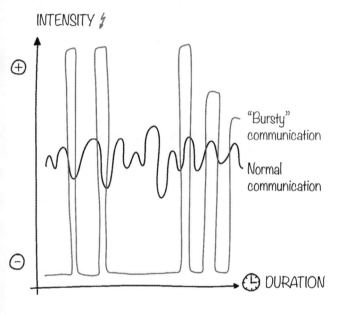

Normal communication = constant background noise. "Bursty" communication = intense activity alternating with total silence.

- "Intensive" communication characterizes exchanges when you are so inspired by your colleagues that your voice veritably cracks with excitement, when you have three ideas all at once, and laugh and clown around. This is also called "bursty" communication.
- "Normal" communication is – well, normal.

The study has shown that when teams engage in rapid-fire exchanges – digitally or in person – they are more creative than teams whose communication culture is "normal." This means that you should arrange set times for "intensive" discussions, or encourage team members to message each other when they're up for a "burst." However, there are a few requirements:

1. Set limits
You can't have rapid-fire exchanges all the time, or for sustained periods. Bursts require set times and a set duration. You should also limit the number of participants: more than four people on one call will drive everyone crazy. Between these bursts, make sure that people are left to immerse themselves in their work, without any interruptions.

2. Mix it up
Interestingly, diverse groups work better than homogenous ones. We tend to prefer working with people who are like us (see *Likeability*, p. 100), but teams that extend you are more dynamic – and therefore more useful – than teams that merely mirror you and your style of doing things. People who are like each other compete with each other, whereas people who differ ultimately inspire each other. One more piece of advice: exclude cynics, pessimists and chronic fault-finders from your team. People like that have a tendency to spot a

problem in every solution. To find out if your team is fit for bursty communication, ask yourself: whose voice carries more weight in my team – those who come up with ideas, or those who quibble with them?

3. Turn off the camera
Facial expressions, gestures, voices, pauses and eye contact are all key to good communication. However, as we discovered during the pandemic, they're difficult to convey over Zoom. Riedl and Williams Woolley suggest that you make burst sessions audio-only, because – interestingly – more people will have their voice heard. Video calls, on the other hand, normally end up with the usual suspects dominating the conversation.

4. Trust
The participants have to feel at ease, safe and respected in each other's company. Only then will they have the confidence to put forward bold ideas, and not take criticism personally.

5. Practice
As with all things in life, practice makes perfect. The more often teams engage in online bursts, the better they will get at them.

INBOX MANAGEMENT: SMART MESSAGING

"Should I always reply to emails straightaway?" is a perennial question in office life. The constant influx of messages – via email and text as well as Slack, WhatsApp, Teams and count- less other messaging apps – is essential to the work we do, but it also keeps us from doing it. In the context of this book, the question is: how can you stop emailing, and start working?

First, the facts: we spend nearly a third of our working day reading and processing messages. (It's been a few years since this study came out, and we can safely assume that today the proportion is even higher.) What's more, a Microsoft study has shown that when you come across someone who is slow to respond to emails, you can be certain that they're an ineffective manager. As organizational psychologist Adam Grant commented, "Responding in a timely manner shows that you are conscientious – organized, dependable and hard- working." Of course, you may still occasionally find yourself having failed to reply to a message, but Grant believes that consistently neglecting your correspondence creates the impression that you're unreliable or, worse, indifferent.

The technical term for the timely handling of messages is "inbox zero," i.e. making sure that there are zero new mes- sages in your inbox. It doesn't mean you have to reply to every email. If the sender asks you a question they can answer themselves, you don't owe them a reply, and the world won't end if you don't respond to an email instantly. However (to quote Adam Grant again): "Not answering emails today is like refusing to take phone calls in the 1990s or ignoring letters in the 1950s." So how can we deal with all those emails without it taking up our entire working day?

Take your time. The sloppier your reply, the more confusion you'll create and the more follow-up questions you'll get. The more considered your response is, the fewer messages you'll have to write, and the better your relationship with the recipient will be.

Learn to say no. If you're asked about something that's outside your area, reply, "I don't know." If you're too busy, say, "I'm afraid I can't take this on right now." If you'd rather not answer the question, reply, "I'd rather not answer that."

Read and reply to messages no more than once a day. This is "yesterboxing" – a technique devised by the entrepreneur Tony Hsieh (1973–2020), whereby you set aside an hour to respond to any emails that have arrived in your inbox in the past 12–24 hours. You'll be surprised to find that many will have already resolved themselves.

The world before and after an important ema|

The world won't end if, once in a while, you don't reply to emails for 24 hours.

KANBAN: HOW TO GET ORGANIZED

We've all had that feeling: you're working on so many projects at once that you don't know where to start; but you do know that you won't complete any of them, because other stuff keeps cropping up.

This type of "to-do overload" often either creates a kind of paralysis ("I'll never get it done!"), or you end up in an exhausting, inefficient whirl of multitasking, where you do a bit of everything but finish nothing. One reason for this is the Zeigarnik effect, according to which planning stresses us out more than execution. (We'll take a closer look at this fascinating effect in *The To-Do List*, p. 66.)

In the 1950s, the Toyota executive Taiichi Ohno (1912–90) came up with a simple technique that can help you to plan less and deliver more, and thus avoid bottlenecks on the production line.

It essentially involves two basic rules:

1. Be transparent to yourself (and others). That is, always be clear about what you're planning **to do**, what you're **doing** right now, and what you've already **done**.
2. Don't despair when faced with big tasks. Parcel them off into smaller ones and make a start on the – now more manageable – subtasks right away. (Plan less, do more.)

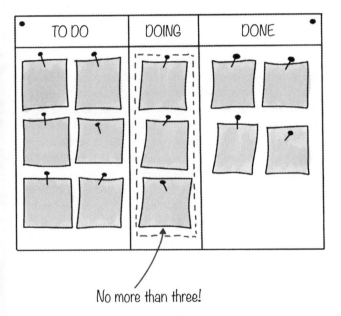

No more than three!

Kanban, the tapas of to-do lists: visualize your tasks, structure them, and complete in stages.

This deceptively simple methodology is called *kanban* (from the Japanese for "signboard"). Once upon a time, it revolutionized Toyota's processes; nowadays, start-ups and small teams regard it as the best approach to structuring work. And that's what's so interesting about it: you can apply it not only to large-scale manufacturing processes, but also on a smaller scale, and to teamwork.

Mark out three columns on a large piece of paper or a whiteboard, and label them "To do," "Doing" and "Done." Look at the projects you need to deliver, and split them into subtasks. For example, the subtasks that make up the project "wedding" would include things like setting the date, deciding on a venue and sending out invitations. Write each of these on a Post-it or index card. Briefly ask yourself, about each subtask: how long will it take? Can I do it myself, or do I need help? Is it more urgent than any of the others?

Attach the tasks to the "To do" column. The *kanban* board helps you visualize the workflow, so as soon as you have started working on a task, physically move it – this is the crucial bit – into the "Doing" column. When the task is complete, shift the Post-it even further to the right, into the "Done" column. Now you're on a roll. You have switched from planning to doing – one of the key elements of *kanban*.

So far, this methodology doesn't look very different from a horizontal to-do list. However, there's one more rule: you're only allowed a limited number of sticky notes in each column. This is called the "work in progress (WIP) limit." It's especially important that you keep your WIP limit for the "Doing" column to a minimum, perhaps no more than three tasks. It's best to work on just one, or a very few, tasks at any given time. That way, your brain can focus all its resources on completing the task in hand, rather than remembering all the open ones. A small number of finished subtasks is more useful than lots of half-done ones. Why? Because the publisher wants to supply finished books, the printer prefers to print finished pages, the typesetter prefers to work with finalized texts and images, and the editorial department prefers to edit a complete manuscript.

THE 5 WHYS METHOD: HOW TO SOLVE PROBLEMS

Just like major catastrophes, everyday problems have both immediate and underlying causes. We often despair at what triggered a problem without understanding what triggered the trigger, i.e. the issue behind the issue. This is where the 5 Whys method can help: you keep asking "Why?" until you've identified the root cause. The key thing is to make sure that you have the right answer to one "Why?" before you ask the next. So whenever you don't know the answer, you should seek advice from other people.

1. Why do my backhand shots always end up with the ball going out these days?
   Because the timing of your groundstrokes is off.
2. Why is my timing off?
   Because you're always a step behind the ball.
3. Why am I always a step behind?
   Because you get out of breath more easily than you used to.
4. Why do I get out of breath more easily?
   Because you aren't training as much.
5. Why am I not training as much?
   Because it's winter.

The brilliant thing about this method is that it exposes answers that are merely superficial and compels us to think more deeply. For this reason, coaches use it to draw out the underlying reasons for our actions.

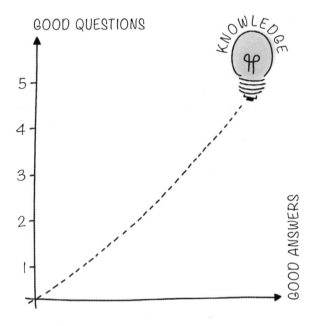

Learning involves give and take: to get the right answers, you have to ask the right questions.

THE 5-SECOND RULE: HOW TO GET STARTED

When your alarm goes off, do you snooze it, or jump straight out of bed?

TV presenter and writer Mel Robbins used to be a "snoozer" – she would hit snooze multiple times, and even turn her alarm off completely. She was also unemployed and had problems with alcohol. Her attitude to life was: it's so shit that there's no point getting up. She knew that she should get out of bed, pour the wine down the toilet, look for a job and work on her relationship. But she didn't.

Robbins calls this the knowledge–action gap. We know what we should be doing, but don't do it. It's a common problem that scientists, for instance, frequently mention in relation to man-made climate change – we know what we could be doing about it, but do nothing. The reason is simple: we like to make things easy for ourselves.

Robbins, too, liked to make things easy for herself, and her personal life was in such a bad state that she preferred to stay in bed rather than think about it. You could even say that she was *procrastinating*, putting things off. It's a widespread problem and has been thoroughly researched. (See p. 6 for some of the reasons why we procrastinate.)

The 5-second rule – useful for doing things you don't want to do.

One day, Robbins remembered the Cape Canaveral count-down before a rocket launch: 5, 4, 3, 2, 1 … Lift-off! The next morning, when once again she didn't feel like getting out of bed, she counted backward, out loud: 5, 4, 3, 2, 1 … and started applying for jobs. She took the garbage out. She went jogging. And then she wrote a book. It's called *The 5 Second Rule*, and is about how counting down changed her life.

This might sound a bit cheesy – and it is. But to ridicule self-help is about as amusing as ridiculing passengers who clap when their plane lands. Robbins's trick is based on a well-known concept in psychology, the "locus of control": that the more we're convinced that we are in charge of our lives, the happier we are. There are two key things you need to know about this:

1. Procrastination isn't liberating – it's draining. A task doesn't disappear because we *don't* do it; we carry it around with us, feel guilty about it and try to ignore it, but it's still there, and we know we have to get it done at some point.
2. Getting (annoying) tasks done gives us a buzz. We all know that little thrill you get when you've tidied up the kitchen, finally changed the bedsheets or filled in your tax return!

However, don't imagine for a moment that you'll enjoy it. To become the person you want to be, you have to force yourself to do things you don't feel like doing. The energy needed for this is called "activation energy," a term that comes from chemistry and describes the minimum amount of energy required to initiate a reaction. In psychology, it describes the energy we require to tackle a task, which can be triggered using the countdown rule.

How do you apply the rule? Instead of thinking too much about whether the technique will work or not, simply try it out for three weeks. Whenever there's something you know you *should* do – for example at night, when you should go to sleep but instead sit up in bed watching Netflix; when you want to go for a jog, but it's miserable outside; or when you're wondering whether to ride your bike or take the car again – execute your own countdown: 5, 4, 3, 2, 1 … and do the right thing.

TRIAGE: WHY YOU NEED A DECISION-MAKING PROTOCOL

Napoleon's early successes during his campaign in Egypt and Syria (1798–1801) ended with the siege of Acre, where a fifth of the French troops died because of a lack of food and supplies. By the end of the campaign, the army had lost a third of its soldiers. Napoleon ordered a meticulous investigation into what had gone wrong. His army surgeon, Dominique Jean Larrey, drily informed him that too many soldiers had succumbed to their injuries in the field because they were treated either too late, or not at all. Larrey proposed using *ambulances volantes*, "flying ambulances," an idea he'd come up with a few years earlier. These were light horse-drawn carriages that enabled first aid to be given to the wounded right away – even as the battle still raged – and meant that they could be transported out of the danger zone and into field hospitals.

The wounded were classified by asking three simple questions:

Will he survive without help?
Will he die despite help?
Will he survive with help?

Anyone in the third group would be treated, regardless of rank or which army they fought for, meaning that enemy soldiers would also receive treatment. Larrey was a humanitarian – he wanted to save lives, not win battles.

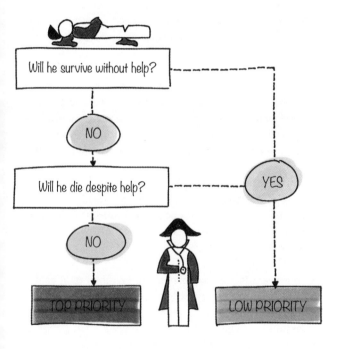

The triage system used in emergency medicine was developed
during the Napoleonic Wars.

This so-called Napoleonic triage system (from the French *trier*, "to sort, select") was first implemented in the battle of Jena–Auerstedt in 1806. It proved astonishingly successful: the mortality rate was markedly lower, and during the battle of Wagram three years later, Larrey saw a 90 percent recovery rate among the wounded in his care. Historians trace Napoleon's immense military success in part to his army's improved medical provision.

To this day, triage forms an essential component of modern medicine – and of business management too, for triage is nothing more than a simple, clear and binding protocol. It's especially useful whenever you are short of resources or time, or when people disagree about how best to proceed.

Here's an example that shows how triage can be applied to marketing. Imagine you're in charge of organizing events. When you receive your first update on ticket sales during the presale phase, you and your team divide the events into three categories:

- The event is a likely sellout. Stop all marketing activity straightaway.
- The event may sell out. Set a budget for further marketing activities and get started on them.
- The event is unlikely to sell out. Stop all marketing and write the event off as a loss – or cancel it altogether if hardly any tickets have been sold.

It's a question of creating binding rules that everyone can stick to, rather than looking at each case individually and thus wasting valuable resources and time. (As anyone who has ever cleared out a basement or apartment knows, you can't consider each object in detail. Instead, create three boxes or piles, labeled "Keep," "Keep till the next clear-out" and "thrift shop.")

Triage frees up valuable space, because you don't have to waste time on basics. It can thus lead to better decision-making, since discussing fundamentals will prove fatal when you don't have all the details and need to act quickly. But be warned: triage is always a trade-off. In order to gain something, you have to give something up. You have to sacrifice one thing so that another can live.

PARALYSIS BY ANALYSIS: HOW TO HOLD YOUR NERVE UNDER PRESSURE

A fox and a cat are arguing about which of them is smarter. The fox says to the cat, "I bet I know more tricks than you." "You may well be right," the cat replies, "because I admit I only know one trick. But my one trick is better than all yours put together." Suddenly, they hear the barking of approaching hunting dogs. The cat climbs into a tree quick as a flash, while the fox stands there, unsure what to do, and seconds later finds himself surrounded by the dogs. "That's my trick," the cat calls down to the fox. "Which of yours did you pick?"

This story is the 605th of Aesop's fables. And its moral? It doesn't actually mean what you think it means – i.e. that all you need is just one good trick. Rather, it shows that while it's all well and good to painstakingly analyze a problem and weigh up all possible solutions, it can prove debilitating in a life-or-death situation.

The US tennis champion Arthur Ashe called the phenomenon when a star player loses their composure – typically after making a mistake – "paralysis by analysis." Even the King of Cool himself, Roger Federer, succumbed to it during the 2019 Wimbledon Final. After two wasted match points, he could have told himself that he was unlikely to lose four points in a row, even against Novak Djokovic. Instead, he became dispirited. Just like the fox in the fable, he had lots of decent options at his disposal to help him out of his predicament – but he lost faith in all of them.

This, then, is what Aesop's fable tells us: during a crisis (or after a failure), don't force yourself to weigh up all the options. Rather, rediscover a cat-like trust in your abilities. There are two ways of achieving this:

1. Change your rhythm. Don't try to force the point – instead, take a step back for a moment. Whether you're sitting at a poker table, negotiating a deal or being interviewed for a job, feel free to take a short break anytime you want. Leave the room, take a few breaths and come back refreshed.
2. Trust the odds. When everything seems to be going against you, tell yourself: "OK, so I might mess up one presentation, one serve, one argument, but surely not four in a row." Statistically, chances are that something good will happen next. If that wasn't true, you wouldn't be where you are today. Have faith.

Aesop's fable of the fox and the cat is about paralysis by analysis
– one of the biggest problems when it comes to decision-making.

THE BOOK OF BOOKS (BOB): HOW TO REMEMBER MORE OF WHAT YOU READ

Whenever we embark on a new venture, we sooner or later end up consulting books on the subject to try to deepen our understanding. Unfortunately, we also forget most of what we read. The "forgetting curve," discovered by the German psychologist Hermann Ebbinghaus (1850–1909), shows that just a day later, we can barely recall a third of what we've read, and in the long run almost none of it. Say you've picked up Adam Zamoyski's *1812*, a powerful account of Napoleon's failed Russian campaign. As you read, you feel you're acquiring a deep understanding of the Napoleonic era. However, two days later you've already forgotten whether Napoleon died on St. Helena or on Elba.

This leads us to the question: if we want to remember more of what we've read, how should we go about reading? There are various ways to do it; this one is our favorite:

1. While you read, underline the passages you think are important.
2. At the end of every chapter, go through the underlined passages. If you still think they're important, write a summary of the key points, or any thoughts they've triggered, on Post-it notes and attach them to the top of the page. When you've finished the book, there'll be lots of Post-its sticking out of it, and all you need to do is glance at them whenever you want to remind yourself of the key points.

3. At the end, write down a brief summary. What is it about? What did I take away from it?
4. Store your notes digitally as well, so that you can find them again via a simple keyword search, even years later.

You should also get yourself a Bob. A Bob? It's a "book of books," where you record which books you've read, and when. You can use a fancy notebook, or do it digitally and publicly. The literary critic Pamela Paul even published hers: *My Life with Bob* gives you an intimate, heart-warming insight into the life of a book-lover, and will prompt anyone who reads it to start their own Bob right away.

A Bob is a great way to remember the books you've read, as well as a lovely souvenir – a reminder of who you were back then, and who you were with.

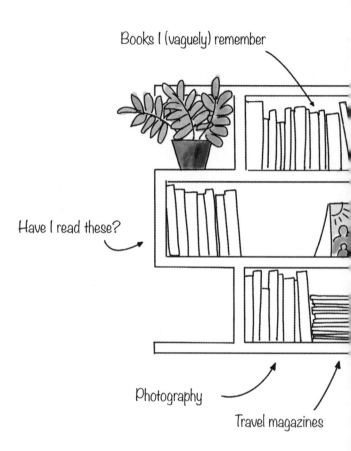

Books I (vaguely) remember

Have I read these?

Photography

Travel magazines

We buy more books than we read, and read more than we can remember. Start your own "reading diary," a book of books.

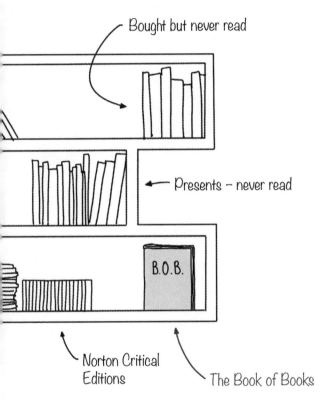

What to do before
you do anything

GETTING A PROJECT DONE: HOW TO START SOMETHING, AND HOW TO FINISH IT

Life is a building site. At least, that's the title of a 1997 German film about how life never turns out as planned but is worth living anyway. You could say the same about projects. They rarely turn out as expected, but where would we be without them? What is certain is that regardless of your job, sooner or later you'll have to carry out a project of some kind. But what exactly does that mean?

Every project is different, but they are all governed by the same parameters: the **resources** (money, knowledge, people) and the **time** you need to achieve a particular level of **quality**. In this book, we propose various ways in which you can approach these three parameters, based on the following seven steps of project management:

1. What do you want to do?
To start with, you need an idea. Inspiration can come from all kinds of sources, such as conversations with other people, immersive reading, long walks, intensive workshops, sheer boredom, revisiting old ideas or a good night's sleep. Ideas show up uninvited, when we're least looking for them. Whenever they do, write them down and chew them over – but never evaluate them right away. For help with this step, see *Bursty Communication* (p. 20), *Brainstorming* (p. 108) and *Structured Evaluation* (p. 114).

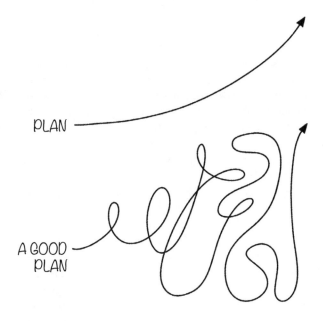

PLAN

A GOOD
PLAN

Everything takes longer than you think. Some things are more difficult than you think. Many won't be as bad as you think.

2. What *exactly* do you want to do, and *why*?

An idea is not the same thing as a goal. "I want to start up a pepper business" is an idea. "I want restaurant X to have my pepper on its tables by this time next year" is a goal. A goal is an idea with a date. For help with this, see *Rapid Prototyping* (p. 16), *The 5 Whys Method* (p. 32) and *The Law of Reversed Effort* (p. 160).

3. How do you want to achieve your goal?

To find out how to arrive at your goal, you first need to know what resources are available. How much time do you have at your disposal? How much money? Who is involved (and who shouldn't be)? What information are you still missing? What can (and can't) you do yourself? As soon as you have clear answers to these questions, allocate your resources, then decide on the necessary action points and put them in the right order. This "right" order will, on closer inspection, usually turn out to be wrong. So you might want to work out what resources you have at your disposal first, and only then refine your ideas and goals (back to step 2). It's annoying when you've planned for a budget of millions which then proves to be nonexistent, or when you discover too late that you can't grow pepper where you live. Perform this step more than once: keep an eye on your resources as you go, and continue to check that they're allocated properly. It's really more like a marriage than a wedding. For help with this step, see *Budgeting* (p. 56), *The Theory of Small Gifts* (p. 104) and *The Circle of Competence* (p. 120).

4. Start working

You'll now most likely be working on your own a lot, or only have occasional, targeted contact with other people. We describe some techniques to help you with this in *Compart-mentalization* (p. 12) and *Deep Work* (p. 72).

5. Give yourself a kick in the pants
Let's be honest: in every project there comes a moment when you hit a brick wall, when you lack motivation or lose faith. At times like these, you need the tools described in *The Pomodoro Technique* (p. 10), *The 5-Second Rule* (p. 34) and *The Transactional Model* (p. 154).

6. Get ready to sprint
There's no way to avoid the scramble to meet the project deadline. Don't trust anyone who tries to convince you otherwise. Parkinson's Law states that "work expands so as to fill the time available for its completion," meaning that the more time you have, the longer everything takes. So gear up early for the final push. You'll find two useful techniques for this in *Kanban* (p. 28) and *The Circle of Influence* (p. 128).

7. Look back (and then ahead)
Regardless of whether or not you achieve your goal, all endings, even unhappy ones, are worth toasting. Then, once the storm has subsided, ask yourself what your journey was like, whether you'd take it again, and what's next. You'll find a helpful technique in *Project Evaluation* (p. 146).

BUDGETING: HOW TO ESTIMATE COSTS ACCURATELY

Top-down estimate

If the project is straightforward or you need to act quickly, do a rough estimate: what will the project cost? Then drill into the detail. How much of your budget will you allocate to each subtask? This method will provide you with a general overview and has the advantage of being quick and easy. The disadvantage is that it's not precise.

Estimate based on experience

If your project is similar to one you've delivered before – i.e. of similar scope and quality – use the costings of the previous project as a guide. Then add 10 percent (everything always gets more expensive).

Approximation

If your estimate needs to be reasonably accurate, work out the likely average cost of each element. How much will it cost at best? How much at worst? And how much in the most likely scenario? An approximation is especially useful if your project is fairly complex.

Bottom-up estimate

Ask subject-matter experts to work out the cost of the individual elements. The sum of these will be your total expenditure. This method is particularly useful for highly complex projects.

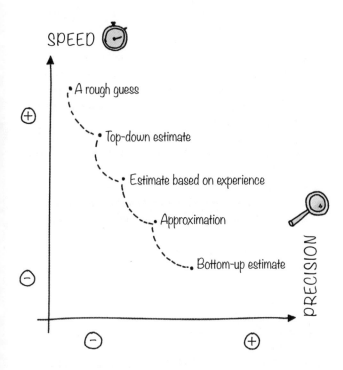

Different ways to estimate – from the quickest to the most precise.

BATCHING: WHEN TO ACT AND WHEN TO HOLD OFF

"Batching" means doing things in bundles. When it comes to doing the laundry, for instance, no one washes each sock individually – we intuitively know that it's more effective to collect a week's worth of dirty socks before throwing them into the washing machine.

But what if you discover a broken roof tile? Should you wait for more tiles to break, or call the roofer to replace the single broken tile immediately? And what if your kid has a tantrum that lasts for days, because the goblins have absconded with their pacifier? Should you do a U-turn or stand your ground?

These are three very different scenarios, but they have one thing in common: they all deal with the question of whether our costs will be linear or non-linear if we delay fixing the problem. If we don't wash a sock right away, the consequences are linear, i.e. they won't escalate exponentially – because all that's required for us to get them under control is to do the laundry. In cases like this, it's worth letting individual tasks accumulate, and then get them done in one go. It's worth batching them.

However, if we don't get that roof tile sorted, the rain might get in, and the whole roof could suffer. The potential costs increase exponentially with each day that we don't do anything about it. In cases like this, batching won't help. We have to act immediately even if things don't look that bad initially.

If your child goes into tantrum mode because you've made them give up their pacifier, the strain on your nerves will be exponential in the short term. But you know from experience that the kid will eventually calm down, and that the pacifier incident won't cause any lasting damage. The problem, in short, will resolve itself – so in this case the best strategy is to hold off and do nothing.

In practical terms, then, if you run into a problem during a project, ask yourself: is it a sock, a roof tile or a pacifier? And then act accordingly.

If you're dealing with a thousand problems at once, I recommend triage (p. 38).

Some problems can be put off (dirty laundry), others have to be dealt with right away (broken roof tile), and others will resolve themselves (pacifier withdrawal).

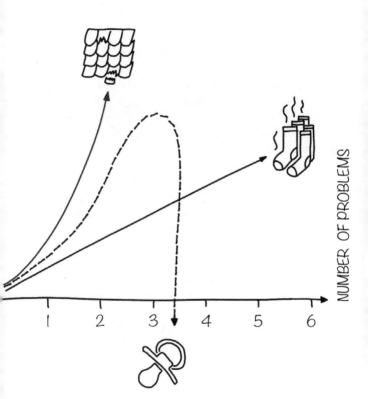

COSTS

NUMBER OF PROBLEMS

THE DELPHI METHOD: THINGS TO BEAR IN MIND WHEN SEEKING ADVICE

Whenever we're faced with a difficult decision, we usually ask a friend – or, even better, an expert – for advice. Which is a good idea, because we all too often let ourselves be guided by emotion rather than facts.

But what if we don't like the advice we're given? Well, we can choose to disregard it. This is a brave thing to do – and often also foolish. It's much better to get a second opinion. So we ask yet another expert and end up with two opinions, which we can then compare. If both experts have given us the same piece of advice, we can assume that it's sound. However, if they disagree, we're left unsure what to do.

When it comes to major, far-reaching endeavors – invasion, capitulation, investments – you can't afford to make a mistake. In the 1950s, the US military developed various strategies to help make their forecasts as accurate as possible, including the Delphi method. The idea is that you ask several experts individually for their appraisal. How outlandish is this scenario? How realistic is that one? Their feedback is then anonymized and taken through a second round, when they are shown their fellow experts' assessments and have a chance to review their own. Even experts don't know everything, don't always consider all the details and can be prone to flawed reasoning – so their colleagues' assessments may draw their attention to a blind spot in their thinking. Other experts'

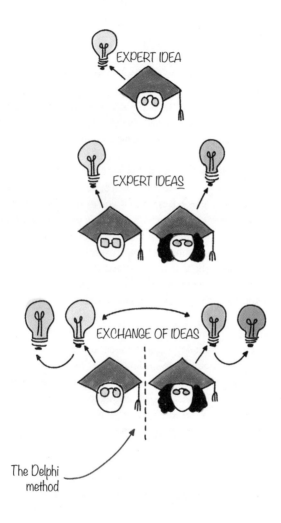

Experts improve their opinions when they're confronted with other ones.

evaluations of a scenario can thus help us revise our own. It's a clever idea.

This method has three advantages. First, you get several different points of view; second, by anonymizing the process you avoid experts discussing the subject among themselves; third – and this is the decisive factor – it gives the experts a chance to question their own opinion without losing face.

These days, the Delphi method is used chiefly in large corporate mergers and international politics, but it also works well on a small scale. For example, if you're considering going freelance, you might ask friends who have experience of this for their advice. But make sure you proceed systematically – that is, once the members of your "expert panel" have given their feedback, share it with the rest of the panelists, and only then decide what to do. This technique is also particularly useful when it comes to cost estimates.

Take another example. Assume you want to open a small concept restaurant in a specific location. If you're serious about it, you probably already know other restaurateurs. Ask them: "What do you think, roughly, will be my turnover per day, month and year?" Once you've averaged out their answers, you'll probably end up with a figure that's much closer to the real thing than the one in your business plan.

Lastly, a few words about asking for advice. Several studies have shown that when we need help, we tend to consult the people we like most, rather than the people who know most about the topic in question. There's nothing wrong with seeking the opinion of a friend who knows you well and wants only the best for you. However, even then the Delphi method can come in handy: as well as your close friend, ask someone who you know is well versed in the subject. Compare the advice you receive. And then show each of them the other person's advice.

THE TO-DO LIST: HOW TO PLAN YOUR WORKDAY MORE ELEGANTLY

The to-do list is one of the oldest human organizational tools. The idea of compiling a list of what you need to do is based on a straightforward logic: when you write something down you don't have to remember it.

This is due to the so-called Zeigarnik effect, whereby our brains are more preoccupied with tasks that we haven't yet completed than with those we've already done. In the 1920s, the Russian psychologist Bluma Zeigarnik (1901–88) observed restaurant staff at work, and found that although they could easily memorize food and drink orders when their customers placed them, once they had served their customers they couldn't recall who had ordered what, even a few minutes later. From this, Zeigarnik concluded that we remember uncompleted tasks better than completed ones. Further studies by her colleague Maria Ovsiankina (1898–1993) revealed that interrupted tasks create in us a strong urge to act (the Ovsiankina effect). Psychologists believe that this also explains why we feel compelled to finish watching a film once we've started, or to read a book all the way to the end.

Taken together, these two effects tell us why to-do lists work so well. If you write something down you don't have to remember it, which leaves your mind free to concentrate on the task at hand (the Zeigarnik effect).

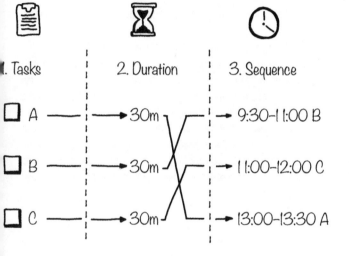

1. Tasks | 2. Duration | 3. Sequence

- [ ] A — → 30m
- [ ] B — → 30m
- [ ] C — → 30m

→ 9:30–11:00 B

→ 11:00–12:00 C

→ 13:00–13:30 A

Don't just list the tasks – plan when you'll do them, and for how long.

At the same time, the list itself is an unfinished task, which is why your brain feels the urge to complete everything on it (the Ovsiankina effect). After all, checking everything off your list is how you prove to yourself that you've achieved something and that your working day is over.

Of course, getting things done is more important than making a to-do list. There are various techniques to help you do this.

One comes from Ivy Lee (1877–1934), one of the most influential management experts of the 19th century. He suggested that, rather than creating your to-do list first thing in the morning, you should decide the previous evening which are the six key things you have to do the next day, and arrange them in order of importance. Then, in the morning, start with the first task, and anything you don't manage to get done goes to the top of the next day's list. That way, you avoid lying awake in bed at night thinking about all the things you have to do tomorrow.

Another variant of the to-do list is called "scheduling," and was devised by the computer scientist Cal Newport (we'll come back to him shortly, in *Deep Work,* p. 72). Newport argues that we should divide our working day into blocks of time, rather than tasks. We usually use our planners to write down appointments that have a specific timeframe or starting point, such as PTA meetings, work meetings or going to the dentist. However, Newport thinks we should assign a timeframe to *everything* we do. This is how:

Start your working day by setting aside defined periods for each task on your to-do list. For instance, two hours for reading a thesis proposal, 40 minutes for a meeting, 30 minutes to prepare your presentation, an hour to go through your emails, an hour for surfing the net and 30 minutes for playing foosball with your colleagues. (Deliberately make room in your day for messing around and time-wasting.)

Make sure that you divide your day into between seven and nine blocks of time at most, and that each block lasts at least 20 minutes. Whatever you're doing, always give yourself the opportunity to get properly immersed in it – and for that you need at least 20 minutes. The long-term goal here is to learn to stick with things, and to get a feeling for how long each task takes.

Now arrange these phases of work in a smart way: progress from the toughest to the easiest, so choose a demanding task for the first one of the day. We concentrate best in the mornings, but we often happily fritter away those hours on replying to emails. Resist the urge.

Of course, when it comes to scheduling – as with all the techniques described in this book – you need to discover what suits you best. If you find that replying to five emails first thing in the morning as a sort of warm-up works for you, keep doing it. But if you catch yourself constantly shifting the more difficult tasks further down the list, you should probably rethink your approach.

MOTIVATION: HOW MUCH SHOULD YOU CHALLENGE YOURSELF?

Imagine you're told to throw small pebbles into a can, and you can choose from how far away you do it. Some people will stand a yard from the can and get the pebble in every time. Others will try it from three yards away and maybe land one in three pebbles. Yet others will stand ten yards away and never get even one in.

The psychologist John Atkinson (1923–2003) argued that the one- and ten-yard throwers are motivated by the desire to avoid failure. They either make things too easy for themselves (because they're afraid to fail), or too difficult (because no one expects you to land the pebble in the can from ten yards away), and whenever the latter unexpectedly succeed they tend to minimize their success. According to Atkinson, the middle group of people – the three-yarders – are motivated by the desire to achieve success, and therefore choose tasks of middling difficulty (not easy, but doable). People motivated by success are proud of what they achieve.

Your attitude to challenge depends on your expectation of success: do you think you can do it? Your expectation of success in turn depends on your previous experience. If you enjoyed success early on in life, you're more likely to expect success again. Ask yourself a question that psychologists often ask people who are facing a significant challenge: "Have you ever passed a test? If so, how did you do it?" That is, try to activate your previous experience of achieving success.

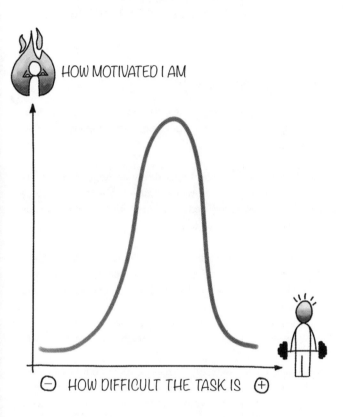

What challenges motivate you? When does difficulty put you off?

DEEP WORK: HOW TO FOCUS DESPITE YOUR SMARTPHONE

Cal Newport, a computer science professor at Georgetown University in Washington, DC, distinguishes between two fundamental ways of working:

- "Deep work": those times when we forget that we are working at all, when we're engaged in an activity that is neither too undemanding (leading to "bore-out") nor too challenging (leading to burnout), and which gets the best out of us.
- "Shallow work": tasks that we find easy, which anyone else could do just as well. This includes drudge work (filling in a table) and routine work (replying to emails, running a software update, collating files). It also includes distractions such as checking Instagram or scrolling through Twitter – activities that thinly slice our attention.

Focusing on one thing for a decent length of time without any interruptions (deep work) makes us more efficient and gives us a strong sense of satisfaction. Conversely, if we keep allowing ourselves to be interrupted (shallow work), we become less engaged, lose concentration and are less efficient. Incessantly hopping from one task to the next distraction creates an attention deficit, where part of our brain is still focused on the old task while we're already dealing with the next. This, says Newport, is not a sound basis for deep work. More complex tasks that require

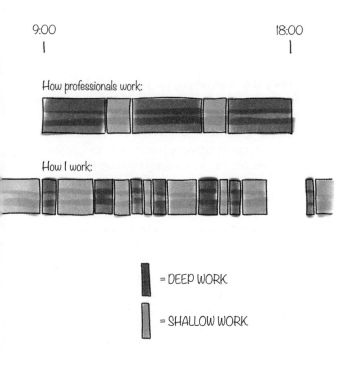

9:00   18:00

How professionals work:

How I work:

█ = DEEP WORK

▌ = SHALLOW WORK

Deep work: immersive, continuous.
Shallow work: erratic, superficial.

intensive thinking – such as developing a new business idea or solving a conflict – are fragmented by all that leaping from one topic to the next. What makes deep work even harder to achieve is that constant distractions are likely to have consequences. If you do "shallow work" for too long, you risk permanently reducing your ability to concentrate.

Here are four techniques to help you attain a state of deep work:

1. Take your time. Block out a chunk of time in your calendar when you'll be immersing yourself properly in a task. (Be warned: we can concentrate at most for four hours a day, but anything less than an hour isn't worth it.)
2. Learn to be bored. In situations when you would normally reach for your smartphone – at the bus stop, maybe, or in the bathroom – try to indulge in boredom instead. Resisting the desire for constant distraction will hone your concentration skills.
3. Look at your social media. Which platforms do you use, and for what? Which do you really need? Keep just one of them. This may have its drawbacks, but what you'll get in exchange is priceless: time. Time for things like deep work.
4. Devise rituals to help improve your concentration. For example, on his writing days, Newport always sits in a particular chair by the window. By doing that, he's telling his brain: "This is where I'll work, not surf online." Whenever he has writer's block, he goes for a walk. When he wants to work on a blog post, he waits until the evening, after he's put the kids to bed, and drinks a beer while he works.

There is no one-size-fits-all solution, of course – you have to find out for yourself what you do and don't need in order to get into "deep work" mode. But find out you must. Your ability to concentrate is what will make you stand out from your rivals.

TACTICS VERSUS STRATEGIES: WHY YOU NEED A STRATEGY (AND SEVERAL TACTICS)

We often use words like "strategy" and "tactics" at work – and get them mixed up. The *Oxford English Dictionary* even lists them as synonyms for each other. But what do they really mean?

A strategy – from the Greek *strategia* ("office of a general") – is the overarching plan we create to achieve our goal. Without a strategy, our life has no direction; we understand neither why we fail, nor why we succeed. As the saying goes, "If you don't have a strategy, you are part of someone else's strategy." If you don't have a plan, you become someone else's plaything. A strategy is not spontaneous or short-lived, but is a long-term answer to the question, "Where do I want to go, and which path will I choose to get there?"

If you want to find out early on whether your strategy is any good, here's a little thought experiment. A time traveler from the year 2030 shows up and tells you that your strategy was wrong. Which part of your plan do you think was the one that failed? Adjust your plan accordingly.

Tactics – from the Greek word *taktike* ("to organize, arrange") – are the individual steps we take as we pursue a strategy.

If you want to give up smoking, your strategy might be to take advantage of a state stop-smoking service. One of your

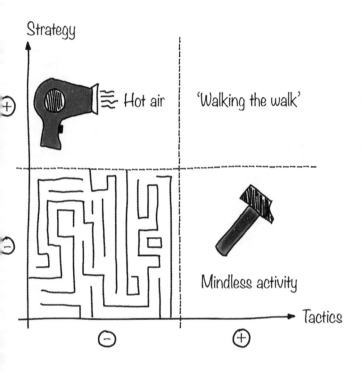

"Strategy without tactics is the slowest route to victory. Tactics without strategy is the noise before defeat." Sun Tzu, 6th century BC (attrib.).

tactics, however, might be to incentivize yourself by posting a message on Facebook saying, "I'll pay $50 to anyone who catches me smoking." Tactics are short or medium term. You can try them out, reject them and adapt them.

Many kinds of tactics have found their way into textbooks and history books, e.g. guerrilla tactics, which is when you lure your opponent into an ambush; salami tactics, where you serve up a proposal slice by slice during a meeting, rather than announcing it all at once with fanfare; and delaying tactics, when commitment-phobes keep their lover on the back burner.

Strategies and tactics are not the same thing, but they go together. A strategy is looking at things from a macro perspective, whereas tactics relate to micro-managing the details. Managers often do one better than the other, but to be successful we need both. We have to be able to see the forest as well as the trees.

Our little diagram shows the complicated relationship between strategy and tactics. If we pursue a goal without a strategy and without tactics, we end up in a labyrinth – wandering blindly through life without a map to show us where our goal is or what awaits us. A good strategy that is never implemented, i.e. doesn't entail specific tactics, is just so much hot air. Working energetically on implementing the wrong strategy often results in mindless activity.

A good strategy needs a set of good tactics to work. As the aphorism often attributed to the Chinese military strategist Sun Tzu goes, "Strategy without tactics is the slowest route to victory. Tactics without strategy is the noise before defeat."

NEW WORK: WHAT DOES IT MEAN TO BE AGILE?

Anyone who has worked for a living in the past 30 years is familiar with the word "innovative." All presentations, briefings, teaching seminars used to include that adjective. Then, about ten years ago, it was replaced by a new word.

Like millions of other employees, Jon Kern was frustrated. Frustrated by rigid processes, long lead times and wrong decisions made early on that couldn't be rectified later. Unlike millions of other employees, though, Kern didn't merely whine about it – he came up with a counterproposal. In 2001, he and his colleagues devised a new way of working, which he called "agile."

What is agile working? It's an attitude rather than a technique. Here's an example:

It's a hot day, and your children need cooling down. You want to drive to the lake, but the car is at the garage. The kids suggest the local swimming pool. But the swimming pool is closed. Fine – in that case you'll have a water-gun fight in the backyard (the kids want to use water balloons).

That's what being agile means.

Your goal was to cool down, but along the way you discovered that plan A (the lake) was a no go – so you got your

(Fr)agile

Solving the
right problem

Solving the
problem the
right way

Agile working is like juggling water balloons: great fun –
assuming everyone's in the mood for it.

"customers," i.e. the kids, involved. They proposed plan B (the swimming pool), but that too was no good. Finally, you came up with an idea together (a water-gun fight), which was completely different from plan A (the lake), but still got you what you wanted (to cool down). The idea is that you make your own path as you walk.

Jon Kern wasn't a nanny, he was a software developer, but the process he proposed was similar: projects would be divided into smaller units, called sprints, and continually adjusted. It means, for example, asking your client or management team for feedback along the way, rather than only at the end.

On a side note, agility is frequently mentioned in connection with "design thinking," a straightforward but far-reaching approach that entails involving as many different people as possible during the development phase. Within the company, you'll involve not only the product development team, but also marketing, logistics, distribution and IT. When it comes to external input, including the end user early on is key. This is why it's also called "user-centered design." In short, involving as many people as possible – clients, colleagues, friends or family – during the problem-solving or creative process will allow you to discover possibilities you hadn't thought of yourself.

In the field of software development, the agile approach is not only considered good manners but is slowly replacing the old-school "waterfall model." According to the waterfall model, you divide a project into successive phases, with the endpoint of one phase forming the starting point of the next. The phases were typically called "requirements analysis" → "system design" → "implementation" → "testing" →

"deployment." In contrast, agile processes involve many more intermediate steps, feedback loops and adjustments. Agile working also implies a more generous attitude: you can't plan reality, because things never turn out as expected. We also don't know what our client wants, but they do. This means that your client is someone who doesn't just sit there and judge your work, but contributes to the process, with their own opinions and invaluable ideas. (Compare *Rapid Prototyping*, p. 16.)

One last thing about agility: a key contributor to its success is understanding that agile teams can and should organize themselves. As a consequence, their way of working can turn out markedly different from that of other teams in the same company, which can cause tension. When you have a good team, the more autonomy it has, the better it gets (whereas a bad team will fail more quickly).

Here are some things to watch out for when trying it yourself:

1. Agile working is challenging. It doesn't suit everyone, but some people will flourish.
2. Certain tasks require agility; others don't.
3. The art is knowing which solutions require agility and which do not.

ROUTINES: WHY YOU SHOULD DO THE SAME THINGS EVERY DAY

The word "routine" makes us think of automatons, boredom and hamster wheels, whereas the word "change" evokes adventure, fresh experiences and people who are open to new things. It's a shame, then, that routines, rituals and traditions are good for our physical and psychological well-being – they provide the predictability and consistency for which we all yearn. Good habits are life's railings: we need places, times and people that we can lean on.

But there's more: daily routines reduce the need to make basic, everyday decisions. The more we can do without thinking, the more efficient we are, and the more energy we have for other things – new, exciting things. So the question shouldn't be "How exciting is your life?" but "What do you do with the time you've gained from having strict routines?"

The thing about routines is that, while they're easy to get excited about, they are also hard to keep up. Doing the same thing day in, day out requires strength, courage and concentration.

This is how you can do it: make a list of your habits, bad and good. Now make a list of the habits you'd like to acquire. Replace two of your bad habits with two things from the new list. Repeat every six months.

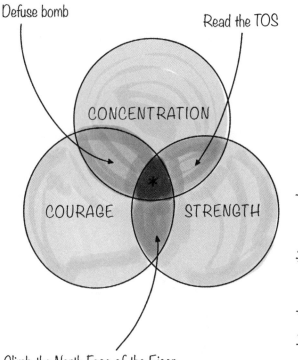

Defuse bomb

Read the TOS

CONCENTRATION

COURAGE

STRENGTH

Climb the North Face of the Eiger

* doing the same thing every day

Sticking to routines is tough. Which three are most important to you?

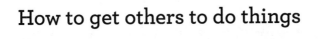

How to get others to do things

APPRECIATION: WHY YOU SHOULD SAY "THANK YOU" RATHER THAN "SORRY'

Picture the following. You are sitting in a restaurant, waiting for your food. It takes a long time to come. Ages. When the waiter finally shows up with it, he doesn't say, "I'm sorry for the long wait." He says, "Thank you for being so patient."

The waiter isn't being snarky, he's being smart. A Chinese–American study has shown that customers who are thanked for their patience rate the restaurant more highly, are more likely to return and more likely to recommend it to their friends, than customers who receive an apology.

So, if you want to get people to do things, it's smarter to thank them than to apologize. Showing appreciation ("thank you") triggers more positive feelings in the other person than asking for their forgiveness ("I'm sorry"). There isn't enough research yet to explain why this is the case, but there are indications that it's to do with affirmation: an apology is about the person who did something wrong, whereas gratitude is about us. We feel better when *we* are made to look good, than when *someone else* chastens themselves. Yet thanking someone instead of apologizing doesn't just make the person you're dealing with feel good, it makes you feel good too. Most people react positively to being thanked, whereas apologies are often received with skepticism, indifference or even condescension. In any case, saying "thank you" is more gratifying than saying "sorry."

Of course, it takes a certain amount of practice to switch from "sorry" to "thank you," but in time it will come to feel normal. Here are a few examples of when and how to do it:

- Your boss discovers a typo in a document you've written. Don't say, "Oh sorry, how silly of me," say, "Thank you for spotting it."
- If you arrive late, don't say, "I'm sorry I'm late," say, "Thank you for waiting."
- When you're with a friend and suddenly realize that you've been hogging the conversation, don't say, "I'm so sorry, I've been doing all the talking," say, "Thank you for listening."

The upshot of all this is: don't constantly apologize, don't keep saying "I'm sorry" – save it for situations when you've treated someone unfairly and sincerely want to beg their forgiveness. On social media, we can't stop ourselves from clicking "Like," sending out hearts and giving instant feedback. But in our offline lives, we often fail to say a simple "thanks." When you work with other people regularly and depend on them, say "thank you" more often, say it sincerely and make eye contact. It'll work wonders.

What do you say when you're late?

Saying "thank you" is more effective than saying "sorry."

RADICAL TRANSPARENCY: HOW TO VALUE CRITICISM

If you work for the asset management firm Bridgewater Associates, you might send the following email to its founder, Ray Dalio: "Ray – you deserve a "D–" for your performance today in the meeting." And Dalio would reply: "Interesting. Tell me more."

This actually happened. When one of Dalio's employees complained that he had acted unprofessionally in a meeting, Dalio emailed the other participants and asked them for their feedback too (it wasn't positive) – and then shared it with the rest of the staff. Why?

One of the principles that Bridgewater lives by is called "radical transparency": a culture of criticism that allows anyone to criticize anyone else – and even demands it.

Its history doesn't take long to tell. In the 1980s, Dalio, then a young investment manager, made a wrong call and almost went bankrupt. Afterward, he decided that whenever he thought he was right about something, he'd ask himself and others: "*Am* I right?" To ensure that everyone would answer honestly, he laid down two rules: (i) there would be radical transparency, i.e. every member of staff should know everything – there would be hierarchies, but no secrets; and (ii) there would be a radical truthfulness, i.e. everyone should be brutally honest, so that people would be less shocked by criticism, and thus learn more.

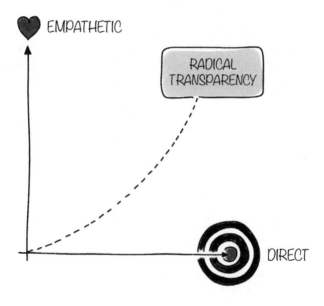

At work, give feedback the same way as you would to a good friend: be direct, honest and considerate.

Briefly, some background. Psychologists have found that criticism instinctively makes us defensive. When someone criticizes us, it hurts, and when we feel hurt, we seek encouragement. So we turn to those people who will reassure us that our critic is an idiot and there's nothing wrong with us. Comfort is good. But does comfort help you improve?

At Bridgewater, they believe that criticism can be extremely useful. They describe it like this: everyone has two voices – one inside their head, and an external voice that says things out loud. Bridgewater wants the two voices to coincide. When we think something, we should also say it. It might sound destructive at first, but in fact it's liberating, because if we are all honest with each other we are no longer left wondering what the other person *really* means or thinks. Instead, we can confront the situation and trust what people say. In this context, expressing criticism means recognizing the other person as an autonomous human being.

We used radical transparency ourselves while working on this book. It was almost killed off by the ruthless criticism we received. But after a while, we realized that criticism can help improve a product; it isn't necessarily just a negative thing that people say to point out your mistakes and show off their own superiority. Admittedly, radical transparency takes some getting used to. Based on our experience, there are three rules to follow:

1. Ask those with whom you want to be radically honest (your partner, team, company, family) if they'd like to try it for a while. Specify a timeframe (a week, a month, the duration of a project) during which you'll engage in radical transparency.

2. Always communicate your criticism as if to someone you care about: be understanding and helpful, and never hurtful.
3. Communicate your criticism straightaway – and be direct. Don't be passive-aggressive, don't wait until years later and don't tell them in a roundabout way.

Afterward, discuss with the others what effect this period of openness has had on you all. If it improved matters, extend the timeframe.

SANDWICH FEEDBACK: DO YOU WANT THE GOOD NEWS OR BAD NEWS FIRST?

If you're an entrepreneur, lead projects or train people – in short: if you "do things" – you will sooner or later be confronted with feedback. A few years ago, the psychologists Angela Legg and Kate Sweeny tried to discover the answer to that age-old question: should you convey the good news first, or the bad news? They found that more than 75 percent of recipients want to hear the bad news first – but nearly 70 percent of news-bearers want to convey the good news first.

In other words, it depends on the situation. On the one hand, there's the news-bearer, who doesn't want to upset the recipient, and therefore starts off with the good news. On the other hand, there's the recipient, who prefers to receive the bad news first, so that they can be comforted by the good news that follows. Both are deeply human behaviors: no one likes to be the bearer of bad news, yet countless experiments have shown that it's the end of a message that lingers – which is why we intuitively want the bad news first, and the good news second.

But the psychologists also discovered that we can influence the recipient by our choice of sequence. First the good news, then the bad, is the best approach if you want to motivate someone to do something ("Your blood test results are fine, but you're overweight"). We emerge from the conversation feeling deflated – which can motivate us to make changes.

First the bad news, then the good, is your best option when you want to bring something to the recipient's attention without demoralizing them ("You've put on weight again, but I love you just the way you are").

The sandwich strategy is a popular extended variant: you communicate the good news first, then the bad, and then another piece of good news. That is, first you praise someone, then criticize them, and then praise them again, so that the conversation ends on a high note. Which is nice for everyone. But sadly also the wrong way to go about it.

For Legg and Sweeny discovered that this sandwich looks better than it tastes. We either wrap the bad news in such tasty praise that the criticism doesn't come across properly, or, conversely, the other person is annoyed because they see through our praise as only so much cheap filler, designed merely to conceal our criticism.

More important than the feedback sequence, though, is the tone and setting. As the author Shane Parrish says: "Make others look good in front of the people they care about most."

GOOD NEWS

An exceedingly tasty warm bun

BAD NEWS

Unmarinated tofu left over from last year

GOOD NEWS

A nicely toasted bottom half

The feedback sandwich: looks better than it tastes.

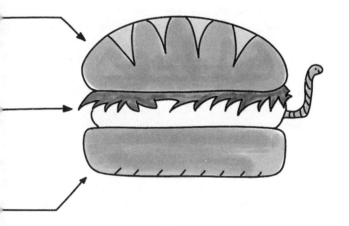

LIKEABILITY: HOW TO WORK WITH PEOPLE YOU DON'T LIKE

Competence and likeability are the two great parameters of teamwork. There's a grid that identifies four distinct archetypes: the competent jerk who's good at everything, but who you don't want anything to do with (the Elon Musk type); the loveable fool, who can't do much but is great company at the bar (the Homer Simpson type); the loveable star who's both clever and likeable (e.g. a unicorn that farts rainbows); and the incompetent jerk (useless as well as loathsome).

These are caricatures, of course, but why don't you give it a try? Put the name of someone from work (or outside work) in each of the quadrants of the diagram opposite. We're quite sure that you'll find someone who fits the bill.

Organizational behaviorist Tiziana Casciaro and her colleague Miguel Sousa Lobo asked participants in a research study which of the four types they would most want to work with. The unsurprising answer was that they all said they would prefer to work with a competent jerk than a loveable fool.

However, our working relationships paint a different picture: likeability is clearly more important to us than competence. "We found that if someone is strongly disliked, it's almost irrelevant whether or not she is competent; people won't want to work with her anyway," Casciaro and Sousa Lobo

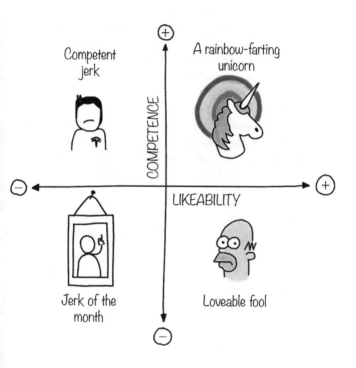

Add your colleagues to the grid. And then yourself.

reported. "By contrast, if someone is liked, his colleagues will seek out every little bit of competence he has to offer."

Does it matter if people prefer to surround themselves with nice if not particularly competent colleagues rather than smart jerks? Yes and no: we enjoy working with people who seem to like us, and when we feel liked we're more open to new ideas, more helpful and more trusting.

But there's a price to pay for working with friends. People who like each other often have similar values and think in similar ways, so as a team they seldom generate fresh ideas. Another problem is that, because most of us avoid competent jerks, their skills frequently remain under-used. It's important to have a mix of types.

What can we do if we're forced to collaborate with someone we don't like? We have to learn to trust them. The reasons we trust someone are rooted in a complex interplay of various factors, the most important of which is similarity: we instinctively trust people who are like us. When someone speaks with the same accent as us, has the same taste in music or went to the same kind of school, we instantly feel an unconscious affinity with them.

So when we ask how it's possible to work with a person we dislike, what we mean is: "How can I learn to trust someone I don't have anything in common with?"

The answer is: remember that they're helping you. Competence alone won't be enough for you to become friends, but once you realize that their skills can help you solve a problem,

the fact that they aren't like you will no longer seem important, and your skepticism will vanish.

So if you ever find yourself in a situation where you want to,
or have to, learn to trust someone you have nothing at all in
common with, show them how you can help them, and simul-
taneously try to find out how they can help you.

THE THEORY OF SMALL GIFTS: WHO SHOULD YOU WORK WITH?

"It's not what you know, it's who you know." This oft-quoted phrase doesn't mean that we should rely only on our connections, but that alone you are no one. Regardless of what we do for a living, networks are indispensable. The problem is: who should we get together with?

A few years ago, Reid Hoffman – the co-founder of LinkedIn and an expert on networks and teamworking – wrote in a blog post that the surest way of finding out what people are really like is to watch how they embark on new relationships. Hoffman believes that we can identify four basic types:

1. "You scratch my back, I'll scratch yours."
The quid-pro-quo approach: "I have to get at least as much out of this as you." People with this approach want an instant return on their investment. Someone like that, says Hoffman, always needs to feel that they're getting something out of it: they don't believe that we're investing in the relationship long-term, because they themselves aren't.

2. "I'll do you a favor, but you owe me one."
People like this are no less utilitarian than those in group one. They're merely prepared to wait longer for their return.

3. "I'm investing in this relationship, and expect you to do the same."

Unlike the first two types, who always keep an eye on who has contributed how much, these people enter into a relationship believing that the other person will do their part.

Types 1, 2 and 3 are fine for a deal or two but are unsuited to a longer-term partnership – they tend to overestimate their own contribution and underestimate their partner's.

4. "I will invest in this relationship because it's the right thing to do."

These people don't expect relationships to yield anything. Your working relationship with them will therefore be more stable than with the other three types. The less we want, the more we'll get. The prerequisite for this kind of collaboration? Trust.

One way to approach this fourth type of person is to show them clearly from the start that you're willing to do your part. In your dealings with them, don't think about what you'll get back – instead, act how you'd like them to act. Hoffman calls this the "theory of small gifts." There are many ways of investing in a relationship without expecting something tangible in exchange. You could, for example, offer to introduce them to other people in your network; bringing the right people together is priceless.

Who would you do a deal with?

Which of these is most like you?

BRAINSTORMING: WHY MORE IS MORE

It's hard to believe, but the word "brainstorming" is only about 80 years old. In his 1948 bestseller *Your Creative Power*, Alex Osborn – the "O" in the BBDO advertising agency, described as a real-life version of *Mad Men*'s Don Draper – argues that a group will generate ideas that would never occur to someone working alone. (Unfortunately, we don't know if the idea came to Osborn during a brainstorming session.)

According to Osborn, successful teamwork is governed by two rules:

1. No criticism. "Creativity is so delicate a flower, that praise tends to make it bloom while discouragement often nips it in the bud."
2. More is more. "Forget quality; aim to get a quantity of answers. When you're through, your sheet of paper may be so full of ridiculous nonsense that you'll be disgusted. Never mind."

Whether or not brainstorming sessions really do produce better ideas has been the subject of numerous studies. The results are contradictory. No, groups of people don't generate better ideas. No, criticism isn't always a bad thing – it can be stimulating. But yes, some people, when they work in groups, come up with ideas they wouldn't otherwise have.

There's something else, too, which Osborn never mentions but anyone who has ever been part of a (successful) brainstorming session is no doubt familiar with: when you develop an idea together, after a while it no longer matters who thought of it first. Instead, you'll discover an unexpected team spirit, genuine enthusiasm and a strong commitment to the idea.

This is how it works in practice: stand in front of a flip chart, and – NO! Stop right there.

While brainstorming sessions usually involve getting everyone to stand in front of a flip chart and wildly yell ideas at each other, there are several problems with this approach: introverted or insecure people will rarely, if ever, vocalize their ideas. In addition, no one in the group wants to look silly, meaning that unconventional ideas usually remain unspoken. Finally, there's the famous phenomenon of groupthink: when one idea proves popular, everyone jumps on the bandwagon, so that there's no room left for other ideas, and the well dries up.

Of course, there are people who spontaneously think of things when they're in a group that would never have occurred to them if they'd been working alone. They should certainly feel free to employ the flip-chart method. For everyone else, however, consider organizing a written brainstorming session ("brainwriting"), where everyone writes their ideas down before the group solidifies, develops and evaluates them. There are three stages to this method:

The analytic stage
During this stage, ask questions that stimulate and channel

everyone's creativity. If you want to rename your company, don't just ask: "What should our company be called?" You need to ask sub-questions. For instance: what potential names are there that have just five letters? Which animal is our company like? What would the company be called if our customers were all teenagers? And so on.

The creative stage

This is when you look for answers. Typically, one question will prompt one or two ideas, which the group then refines. However, that's the wrong way to go about it: the first couple of things that spring to mind are usually the most conventional, which is why we think of them first. But only a few people can come up with more than two different answers when faced with a blank page. There are various techniques you can employ at this point to help generate fresh ideas, such as:

- Answer question 1 on the spot. Don't sit down, and don't spend a lot of time on it.
- Answer question 2 on a sheet of paper. Write down a rough outline of your idea and pass the sheet to the next person, who then completes the answer by adding further details.
- Answer question 3 in 15 minutes using Google.
- Answer question 4 visually: make a collage from old newspapers (or sketch something by hand).

The critical stage

This is when you solidify the ideas, and then filter them. Only workable solutions make the cut. If the question is "How do we market our new organic label?," "likeability" isn't an idea but a wish. To make ideas easier to compare, they should be

consistent: title, subtitle, a representative image or explana-
tory sketch, and a 100-character description.

And now? Read on to find out how to evaluate the ideas
you've developed, and then choose the right one.

Every introvert's nightmare: coming up with ideas in a group setting.

STRUCTURED EVALUATION: HOW TO COMPARE IDEAS

You're probably familiar with this scenario: you've had a (good) brainstorming session, and there are lots of (good) ideas on the flip chart. The energy level is high. But now what do you do? How do you decide between them?

First, you should be aware that the question of which idea to pursue and which not – and especially how to get everyone to agree on this – is a minefield. At this point, any number of things can go wrong. You might be too compromise-happy and turn three good ideas into one bad one ("Let's do a combination of them"). Or you might settle on an idea for tenuous reasons ("This one feels right"), or rub everyone the wrong way by being too bossy ("This is what we'll do"). An even more popular next step is to postpone the decision until you've brought in an expert ("I want to go home first and show it to my dog/my five-year-old"). As a rule, the high energy level will give way to passive-aggressive frustration.

Here's a little technique that we've often used ourselves to evaluate ideas – and which can help you, too, by providing a more solid foundation than simply handing out dot stickers.

When you develop ideas as a group, you should also evaluate them as a group. (However, this doesn't mean that the final decision has to be democratic. Quite the opposite: if a leadership team is involved, it's crucial that they make the

(The boss – double weighting?)

(Polarizing idea)

	Karen	Arthur	Regina	μ	σ
IDEA 1				6.3	3.9
first impression	1	9	9	6.3	
practical?	2	7	10	6.3	
IDEA 2				5.8	2.5
first impression	6	7	10	7.7	
practical?	4	5	3	4.0	
IDEA 3				6.5	0.5
first impression	6	7	6	6.3	
practical?	7	6	7	6.7	
μ	4.3	6.8	7.5		

(Regina is the most generous judge)

Don't discuss – evaluate. A sample idea-evaluation grid.

decision. But before that, everyone should have a chance to evaluate the ideas.) That way, whichever group or individual ends up making the final decision will receive an initial recommendation that's broadly supported by the whole group. It will also break down hierarchies, which almost always hinder progress.

To evaluate the ideas properly, bear in mind two things:

1. The ideas should be formulated and presented equally. This is difficult, but crucial. By "equally," we mean that they should have roughly the same amount of meat on their bones, and also look the same (i.e. either all ideas should be accompanied by visuals, or none).
2. Never compare more than seven ideas, or you'll lose track. If there are more than seven on the table, draw up a shortlist.

Now assess the ideas using two, or at most three, para-meters. Think back to the beginning of the creative process. What problem are you trying to solve? What was your starting position? What were the criteria? These will provide the parameters for the evaluation process. For example: "On a scale from 1 to 10, how successful is the idea likely to be?" Or: "How realistic is it?" "How new is it?" "How quickly can we implement it?"

For what comes next you need a little Excel know-how. Create an Excel table that includes the names of the participants, their ideas and your parameters (see illustration). Work out the average (the mean) and the standard deviation for each idea and parameter.

Now present the first idea. Each person in the group has 30 seconds to write down their ratings on a piece of paper (one rating for each parameter). Then ask everyone to read out their ratings, while someone adds these to the table. Then evaluate the next idea.

When each idea has been rated, ask the participants to rank them from best to worst. Add their rankings to the table.

After a short break, move on to the discussion phase. Which ideas have a high average (mean) rating? Which have a high rating for just one parameter? Which ideas are polarizing (high standard deviation)? What is also interesting is seeing who has given mostly high or mostly low ratings. Finally, which idea sticks out if you only take the overall rankings into account?

Finally, complete this evaluation exercise by putting together a written recommendation, which you'll then pass on to the decision-maker.

Doing things differently

THE CIRCLE OF COMPETENCE: WHY YOU SHOULD SAY "I DON'T KNOW" MORE OFTEN

The "circle of competence" is a well-known thinking tool that helps you do the right thing and avoid doing the wrong thing. We don't know where it originated, but the investor Warren Buffett popularized the concept when he used it in his 1996 letter to the shareholders of Berkshire Hathaway:

What an investor needs is the ability to correctly evaluate selected businesses. Note that word "selected": You don't have to be an expert on every company, or even many. You only have to be able to evaluate companies within your circle of competence. The size of that circle is not very important; knowing its boundaries, however, is vital.

What did Buffett mean by this? What he meant was that we shouldn't invest in something we don't understand, and that we need to be able to distinguish between what we know and what we don't know. Someone who claims to know everything is no less a fool than someone who knows nothing.

This principle is useful even if you don't particularly care for the wisdom of rich old white men – you don't have to be a stock exchange investor. When you have a quiet moment, work out your professional circle of competence. Ask yourself: "What *is* my field of expertise? What do I know a lot about?" Or: "What would I like to be an expert in?" It's not so much a question of becoming an expert in a specialist

I DO KNOW <u>THIS</u>.   I DON'T KNOW <u>THIS</u>.

"I don't know" is one of the most important things you'll ever say.

field, as of knowing more about a subject than the next person. It's a question of taking something you can already do and becoming as good as possible at it – rather than expending a lot of blood, sweat and tears on something you can't do, in order to achieve mediocrity.

There are two exceptions to this. First, young people don't need to create a circle of competence yet. It's detrimental to specialize too early. Instead, you should try your hand at this and that, fail, and start again. It's the only way to discover your passion in life. Second, the circle of competence is relevant only to your job. In your personal life, you should do whatever brings you joy, even if you aren't very good at it.

We automatically start creating our circle of competence a few years into our working lives, but are we doing it consciously? Do you know the limits of your circle of competence, i.e. what is and isn't in your area? Does your circle of competence correspond to your skills, and are you ready to stay inside it?

Maintaining your circle of competence requires two things. First, you have to focus. To become a true specialist you need a fair amount of willpower and discipline, almost a certain obsessiveness. Second, learn to say no. Your time is limited, and there's only so much you can absorb. You can't take on everything, jump on every bandwagon and have an opinion on every topic. However, your circle of competence is by no means static. It's in constant motion because there will never come a time when you know enough. What makes competence both difficult and such a pleasure is that even an expert has to learn something new every day.

Above all, understanding your circle of competence means not deceiving yourself or others by talking about things you hardly know anything about, or by applying yourself to something you'll never master anyway. Instead, get used to saying "I don't know" when you don't know something. Paradoxically, this will make others trust you: by confessing your ignorance, you're showing that you're aware of your circle of competence. And the more you know what you don't know, the more inquisitive you'll be – and the more receptive to people who *do* know.

But how can you find out what your circle of competence is? How do you decide what to focus on, which field to immerse yourself in? For this, you need the 5/25 rule, which we'll turn to next.

THE 5/25 RULE: HOW
TO AVOID REGRET

"Have I fulfilled my potential? Have I spent my life doing something I really love? Have I got my priorities right?" These are some of the tough questions we often ask ourselves around the time we hit the age of 40.

The 5/25 rule helps you make sure that, at the end of your life, you're more likely to answer "Yes" to all three questions than "No." The method has been (wrongly) ascribed to Warren Buffett – but it doesn't matter who came up with it. What's more important is its impact: some people claim that it will change the way you look at your life for ever.

Why don't you try it?

Step 1. Write down 25 things you want to achieve in life. It doesn't matter what they are: learn Spanish, become a better person, climb Mount Everest, enjoy your job more, earn more money. (You can start small, and instead write down the 25 things you want to do in the next year.)

Step 2. Look at your list and highlight the five most important items. (If you're doing the exercise right now, take your time to complete the first two steps before reading step 3.)

Step 3. You now have two groups: the five goals you've high-lighted are group A, and the 20 goals you haven't highlighted are group B. Look at the goals in group B. They aren't just any old goals, they mean something to you. Look at them again. And then cross them out. Never think of those 20 goals again. They're important but will only distract you from the other five. More than that: they'll keep you from achieving your five most important goals.

Step 4. Look at the goals in group A. Now devote your life to these five – and only these five. They will become your circle of competence (see *The Circle of Competence*, p. 120).

The 5/25 rule is all about managing opportunity costs: what will you miss out on, if you eliminate lots of possibilities and focus on just a few? What happens if you don't keep all your options open, or don't hold out for something better? In short, is it so bad to learn to say no? You can't do everything, know everything or be everything, so it's better to focus on only one thing, and truly master it.

Love springs from devotion, not attraction. Immersing yourself in something is the surest way never to lose heart.

25 THINGS I WANT TO DO WITH MY LIFE

1. Buy an apartment
2. Open a small museum
3. Spend more time with friends
4. Put the kids first!
5. Hike the Appalachian trail
6. Learn Farsi
7. Total career change
8. More sex (or better sex)
9. Write a screenplay
10. Buy nothing for a whole year
11. Never fly again
12. Build a tree house

13. Forgive my parents
14. Draw well
15. Grow asparagus
16. NYC marathon
17. Mentor someone
18. Brew my own beer
19. Wimbledon (visit)
20. Laugh more! ☺
21. Get a lot less annoyed
22. Concert at the Elbphilharmonie
23. Stay pain-free
24. Get fitter & faster
25. Talk less, listen more

Which five goals do you really want to achieve?

~~3~~ 5 THINGS I WANT TO DO WITH MY LIFE

~~1. Buy an apartment~~

~~2. Open a small museum~~

3. Spend more time with friends

~~4. Put the kids first.~~

5. Hike the Appalachian trail

~~6. Learn Farsi~~

~~7. Total career change~~

~~8. ~~More~~ sex (or better sex)~~

~~9. Write a screenplay~~

~~10. Buy nothing for a whole year~~

~~11. Never fly again~~

~~12. Build a tree house~~

~~13. Forgive my parents~~

~~14. Draw well~~ → (Generally learning)

~~15. Grow asparagus~~

~~16. NYC marathon~~

17. Mentor someone

~~18. Brew my own beer~~ → But more tennis

~~19. Wimbledon (visit)~~

~~20. Laugh more!~~ ☺

21. Get a lot less annoyed

~~22. Concert at the Elbphilharmonie~~

~~23. Stay pain-free~~

~~24. Get fitter & faster~~

25. Talk less, listen more

THE CIRCLE OF INFLUENCE: WHAT YOU CAN AND CAN'T CHANGE

One of the truest and most inspirational statements about life – whether you're religious or an atheist (or aspire to be one or the other) – comes from the American theologian Reinhold Niebuhr (1892–1971). His famous Serenity Prayer goes like this:

God, grant me the serenity to accept the things I cannot change, the courage to change the things I can, and the wisdom to know the difference.

The author Stephen R. Covey explores the prayer's core idea in his 1989 personal development book *The 7 Habits of Highly Effective People*. The title lays it on a bit thick, but don't let that put you off – it's a classic that has sold more than 40 million copies worldwide and is well worth reading. Covey's book includes a fantastic exercise called "circles of influence and control." This technique can help whenever we feel ineffectual, powerless or frustrated.

This is how you do it. Draw three concentric circles on a piece of paper, just like the illustration opposite.

The outer circle is the "circle of concern." Add to it the things that bother you but you can't do anything about, such as Covid-19. The coronavirus pandemic has caused serious issues worldwide and everyone's been affected by it, but none

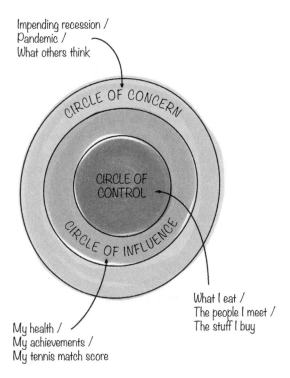

Impending recession /
Pandemic /
What others think

CIRCLE OF CONCERN

CIRCLE OF
CONTROL

CIRCLE OF INFLUENCE

What I eat /
The people I meet /
The stuff I buy

My health /
My achievements /
My tennis match score

Knowing what we can and can't control is an immensely powerful tool.

of us can solve these sorts of crises single-handedly. We're quite helpless.

Other things that belong in this circle include any events that lie in the past, e.g. episodes from our childhood, or concerns about the political climate, impending recession or natural catastrophes, or specific issues like other people's flaws, or what others think of you. You have no control over any of these, so this is where they all belong.

The circle at the center is the "circle of control." Think about the things in your life that are in your hands. They're often trivial things we rarely think about, but they have a huge effect on us – such as the foods we eat, the people we meet, the books we read, and the films we watch. Add them all to the circle.

There's immense power in knowing which things in our lives we can and can't control.

Now let's look at the middle circle, the one between the circle of concern and the circle of control. This is your "circle of influence." That's where you put whatever isn't in your hands, but which you might be able to influence through your attitude or behavior.

You can't single-handedly avert climate change, but you can do something about it by living sustainably; you can't change your genes, but you can exercise regularly and eat more healthfully. And here's a third example: you have no power over the events in the circle of concern, but you can influence, and even control, your reaction to them.

What do we learn from this exercise? The more you focus on things you can't influence – i.e. the ones in the circle of concern – the more helpless and ineffectual you'll feel. But the more you focus on the things that are in your hands – those in the circle of control and circle of influence – the more confident and less anxious you'll be.

DISRUPTIVE INNOVATION: WHY AIRBNB IS REPLACING HOTELS

A question every entrepreneur asks themselves is: "How can I make more money?" Yet only a few entrepreneurs ask themselves: "Have I missed an innovation?"

At least, this is the view of Clayton Christensen, probably the single most influential business consultant of recent years, who died of leukemia in 2020 at the age of just 67. In his work, Christensen devoted himself, among other things, to finding out why industry leaders have historically failed to take advantage of practically every trailblazing innovation.

Here are a few examples: Nokia once dominated the cell phone market, but failed to make the most of smartphones and was eventually overtaken by Apple; the big players in the music business were shown up by Napster and the retail industry by Amazon; movie theaters have been overshadowed by streaming platforms like Netflix; and hotel chains are being outdone by Airbnb.

Christensen distinguished between "sustaining innovation," i.e. improving existing products, and "disruptive innovation," i.e. launching new products or new technologies, rewriting the rules of the game. Established companies usually try to improve already successful products (sustaining innovation) so that they can charge even more for them. But often their customers haven't asked for any performance enhancements.

133

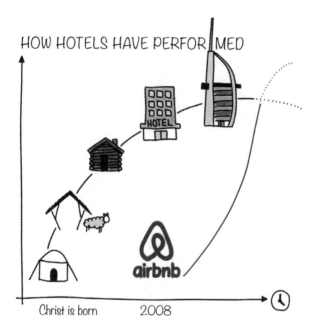

HOW HOTELS HAVE PERFORMED

Christ is born   2008

The hotel industry prospered for millennia. Then, in 2008,
Airbnb appeared.

Christensen called this "overshooting": the company's management ignores the customers' needs and overshoots its target. This is what happened with the Burj Al Arab hotel in Dubai: yes, erecting the tallest building in the world has always held a certain fascination, but is it what hotel guests want? Meanwhile, disruptive innovations quietly emerge to outflank the market leader with a product that is not merely better but a different product altogether. They change the rules of the market. In the case of hotels the disruptor was Airbnb, with its idea of turning homes into vacation rentals.

Generally speaking, anyone who has spent years in charge of something wants to see as little change as possible. They're reluctant to introduce anything new so long as things are bubbling along fine, whereas disruptive entrepreneurs try to create something new – and often take huge risks, because they have less (or nothing) to lose.

Established firms usually first ignore and then ridicule a newcomer, simply for offering something different. Yet while they're busy mocking the disruptive innovation, it gains market share. Now they start taking it seriously and try to fight it off – or buy it – and eventually the innovators remove the established firms entirely from the equation.

Disruptive innovations don't necessarily involve radically new or different technology: their key quality is that they are *not* "sustaining." That is, they don't subscribe to the same market logic and value systems as the old players. In the case of Airbnb, the tech solution was nothing to write home about, but the basic idea – people renting out their homes – represented a radical break with the hotel industry's market logic and value system.

Christensen said that the innovator's great dilemma was that, although improving an existing product can significantly increase your profits in the short term, in the long term you risk being overtaken by a new development. Betting on a potentially disruptive innovation, however, is an unquantifiable risk because it may not succeed (hello, Google Glass!).

This is how you do it. As you plan your next 12 months, don't just ask: "How can my best cow produce even more milk?" Also ask yourself: "What, in my industry, is the equivalent of oat milk?" Or: "What idea did I smile at condescendingly two years ago, which suddenly looks like it's catching on everywhere?"

KOTTER'S 8-STEP MODEL OF CHANGE: WHY CHANGE IS TOUGH

Whether you're running a household or a big corporation, there will always come a time when you want, or need, to change something – be it processes, the rules of the game or your overall strategy. In 1996, John Kotter, a thought leader in business and management, argued that the reason we meet resistance whenever we want to implement a change is that most people experience change as a threat.

Kotter devised an eight-step process that is nowadays considered the gold standard in modern change management. It may look dull at first glance, but really isn't; and you can apply it even to small-scale changes and changes to your personal life.

1. Create a sense of urgency
Explain why the change is necessary – not just for you personally or for the company, but for everyone who works there. The reason why people are sometimes so resistant to change is that its essential usefulness hasn't been made clear enough. Kotter argues that if you want change to succeed you generally need 75 percent of staff to buy into it.

2. Build a guiding coalition
Don't try to push a change through on your own. Instead, put together a coalition and set up a "change team" with members recruited from across all departments. The idea is

$$\text{Change} = \frac{\text{Desire for something new}}{\text{Fear of the new}}$$

to ensure that as many staff as possible feel that they and their concerns are represented during the process.

3. Formulate a vision
"Better quarterly results" isn't a vision, it's a goal. "Effective innovation and dynamic development" isn't a vision, it's verbiage. A vision has to be credible and practical, ambitious yet achievable. It needs to be a statement that 75 percent of your colleagues can buy into.

4. Communicate your vision
And don't merely communicate it on launch day. Ask yourself whether your day-to-day actions also reflect the vision.

5. Remove obstacles
Any change requires a certain amount of effort and sacrifice. If anyone is reluctant and keeps trying to sabotage the process, you need to change their mind, integrate them, or (as a last resort) remove them from the process.

6. Generate short-term wins
If you're planning a major change, you'll inevitably go through long dry spells, when it looks as if the goal is receding into the distance or even slipping out of reach. At these times, it's important to create some quick wins in the midst of the seemingly never-ending slog. Even if the project isn't running smoothly as a whole, there will be some things that are going well. Make sure that, along the way, you always make your colleagues feel that they're on the right track. Reward especially those who are supporting the change process.

7. Stick with it

You'll only know if a change works if you've tried out the new configuration.

8. Embed the change

If you don't, there's a risk that it will be reversed the moment the pressure lets up, or when you leave the company.

A NEW MAP OF LIFE: WHY YOU SHOULDN'T START WORKING UNTIL YOU'RE 40

Ask any of your friends or family aged between 35 and 55 what they lack most, and most of them will probably mention something directly or indirectly related to "time." They would like more "me time," more time to spend with their children or partner, more time for work, more time for hobbies. The work–life balance is an important issue for many of us, but we simply don't have enough time for everything. Or rather, we do – we just haven't been arranging our lives properly.

Laura Carstensen, the founder of the Stanford Center on Longevity in California, has made the following observations – which aren't as trivial as they seem:

- We're getting older. Today, a 40-year-old woman will on average live another 45 years, and a 40-year-old man will live another 42 years. And counting.
- We're getting healthier. Many 65-year-olds are fit enough to work, and want to – but there are no jobs for them to do.
- We're still living our lives according to models that assume a much shorter lifespan.
- The traditional three-step life plan – education, work and family, retirement – is outdated.

Even now, we still try to get all our education out of the way early on; then, perhaps, we'll start a family, as we work till we

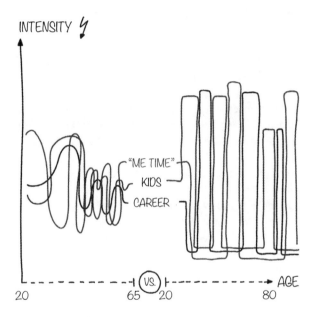

It's a good idea to do one thing at a time, instead of everything all at once. At least, it's better that way on a graph.

drop, expecting all the while to retire in our sixties and die ten years later.

In the 20th century, average life expectancy rose by 30 years. But instead of asking ourselves how we can make use of those 30 years – for example, by improving life on this planet – we have simply added them to the end.

Carstensen claims it's time that we seriously considered a wholesale redesign of life. This is why, a few years ago, she launched the New Map of Life initiative. It's not an instruction manual so much as a call to action for all kinds of academic disciplines, urging them to consider the demands of a society where people will live to an average age of over a hundred.

Instead of a breathless sprint, Carstensen proposes a steady marathon. That is, don't try to do everything at the same time when you're between 20 and 65 years old – instead, tackle one thing after another between the ages of 20 and 80. There will be times when you'll power ahead at work, and times when you'll dial things down; times when you'll undergo further education or retrain, and times when you'll focus on your children.

Maybe you'll have children first, then go to college, and then enter the job market – mature, but hungry. Or maybe the other way round: you'll embark on a career first, then slow things down to have children, and then switch your focus back to your career again.

Carstensen's model is based on two premises:

1. An end to our obsession with youth. Carstensen urges a rethink: what skills do older people have that are missing in our businesses and society at large?
2. An end to our obsession with speed. If we're going to work till we're 80, we must make sure we don't hit burnout long before then.

If you like the idea of a New Map of Life, how can you put it into practice?

You could seek out projects that support this kind of initiative. For instance, in Switzerland there is a network called ting.community, where members share not only their expertise but also their money. Everyone pays into a communal pot each month, and if (for example) you want to set up a new business or retrain, you can ask the community to finance it. If such a thing doesn't exist where you are, you could set one up. Or if you're in the personnel department, set aside a little time to investigate whether there are any parts of your business where older staff could work. You could also consider multi-generational living.

Most importantly, though, the sooner you get used to the idea that you have a long life ahead of you – and will have to fill it *somehow* – the better.

What to do with the
things you've done

PROJECT EVALUATION: HOW TO ASSESS YOUR OWN WORK

The classic way of judging whether something has been a success is this: you set a goal that you want to achieve in a certain amount of time, and if you achieve the goal within that timeframe, you've succeeded. You're thus working with two parameters: the scale of your success and its relation to time.

Take, for example, a group of students who are working together on a project that's due on a certain day. You (the professor) don't care how they do it. They might experience lots of highs and lows along the way, fall out with each other, and finally complete the project only after pulling an all-nighter, swearing never to work together again – you don't care. All you're assessing is the quality of their work, and whether they handed it in on time. Meanwhile, another group, who worked well together and enjoyed the work, hand their work in late. You fail them because even though they achieved the goal, they took longer to get there. What you're assessing is the project, not the process.

Over the past 20 years, we've come to realize that this is the wrong approach to project work. If we evaluate a project based only on whether or not we reached our goal, without reflecting on how we did it and what we could have done better, we're wasting professional as well as personal learning opportunities. If we only ever ask, "Did we achieve our

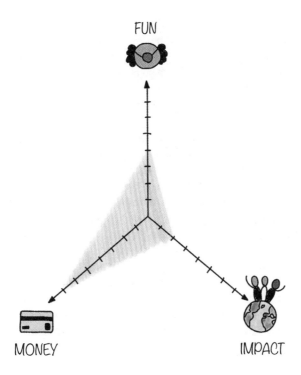

FUN

MONEY

IMPACT

Fun, money, impact – you need at least one of them.

goal?," we learn neither from our successes nor from our failures. What we also need to ask is, "How did we get there, and do we want to do it the same way next time?" In other words, we have to reflect on the process.

Good questions about the process include: which approach did we choose? How did we reach decisions? How did we handle periods of tension? Who played what role? Which role was missing? Of course, we have to evaluate the product, but there are other important assessment criteria too.

In the short to medium term, a good product is crucial. A good process, however, will have a long-term impact. A good product affects the quarterly figures, whereas a good process affects your corporate culture. Staff who leave a company don't do so because they dislike the product, but because they can no longer tolerate the company's work culture and atmosphere.

Now, there are various ways to evaluate a process or a project, but many techniques are so laborious that they themselves start looking like a project in urgent need of assessment. Over the past few years, we've found the following evaluation technique particularly useful – and it takes no more than 30 minutes.

The starting point is our hallowed triumvirate of fun, money and impact. At the end of a project, we ask these three questions – about the outcome as well as the process:

1. Was it fun?
2. Did we make money from it?
3. Has it had a positive impact (on us or other people)?

Three yeses are heaven; we'll settle for two, but one yes is the minimum we need if we are to repeat the project. If there isn't even one yes, this type of project or process goes on the not-to-do list.

THE MYTH OF ACHIEVEMENT: HOW MUCH OF YOUR SUCCESS IS DOWN TO LUCK?

As this book is called *To Do* we should briefly discuss "achievement." The more successful we are, the more we're inclined to put our success down to sheer hard work and hide the fact that we probably enjoyed a fair tailwind on our journey. Such as from our parents, who helped us through school or got us a job. However, what makes the biggest difference is the country you're born in. If someone is born in Lesotho, they're unlikely ever to become as well off as a child born in the US, no matter how talented and hard-working they are. If we ignore this tailwind, convinced that our effort alone determines how far we get in life, what we're really saying is that it's entirely your own fault if you don't make it.

Don't misunderstand us: nothing comes from nothing, and even successful people have had to work hard for their success. But always remember that many people never make it, no matter how hard they work. Acknowledging the fact that coincidence has played a part in your achievements isn't to say that you haven't earned your success: all it means is that there are lots of others who deserve success just as much, but who haven't been as lucky as you.

WHY WE ~~THINK WE~~ ARE SUCCESSFUL

How much of your success has been down to luck?

THE MATTHEW EFFECT: WHY YOU SHOULD CELEBRATE YOUR TRIUMPHS

"Whoever has will be given more," says the Gospel of St. Matthew. "Whoever does not have, even what he has will be taken away from him."

We all know that a single foolish act can result in another: you get into debt, and then get into more debt in order to clear the first debt. But the converse is also true: if we're given an opportunity and seize it, two more opportunities will come our way, and then another four.

The US sociologist Robert Merton (1910–2003) popularized the idea of the Matthew effect when he discovered that famous scientists were more frequently cited in scientific publications than lesser-known researchers – which made the famous scientists even more famous. This principle is valid in both economics (the widening gap between rich and poor) and psychology (success breeds success).

What can we do about this? We know that when a pupil finds a subject difficult, they work less hard and get worse grades. Pedagogues recommend that we build children's self-confidence by always also giving them a task that they *can* do. Applied to your adult life, it means skiing down the broad blue trail now and again, instead of always down the steep black one. What motivates us is success, not failure.

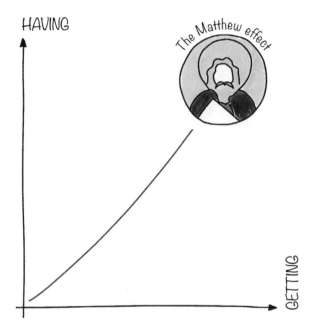

HAVING

The Matthew effect

GETTING

"Whoever has will be given more ... Whoever does not have, even what he has will be taken away from him." (Matthew 25:29).

THE TRANSACTIONAL MODEL: WHAT TO DO WHEN YOU RUN OUT OF ENERGY

Have you ever felt on the verge of being overworked, tired and irritable? We're not talking about actual collapse, but the feeling you get just beforehand – when you know you'll suffer burnout if you don't do something about it. The transactional analysis theory, developed by Canadian psychiatrist Eric Berne (1910–70), calls this a loss of mental energy.

Psychological needs are equivalent to physical hunger, and Berne argued that, just as your body requires energy in the shape of carbohydrates, fat and protein, your psyche also requires energy. It needs it in the shape of structure, stimuli and recognition. Using the model on the page opposite, you can perform a quick check on your own energy reserves.

Pick up a pencil, copy the model into your notebook, and create a snapshot using a scale from 0 (needs improvement) to 10 (completely happy).

1. Structure
To what extent is my need for clear processes, binding agreements and good time management being satisfied? Adults are nothing if not former children: we need strict rituals and processes to feel at ease.

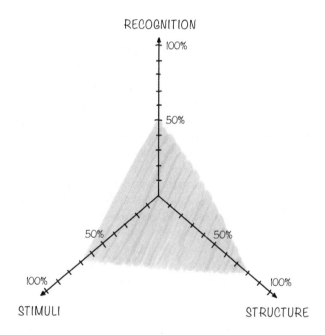

How much structure do you need at the moment? How much input? How much recognition?

2. Stimuli

To what extent is my need for mental nourishment, new perspectives and fresh stimuli being satisfied? This is partly about intellectual input, but – at a time of digital living and remote working – also partly about "real" contact.

3. Recognition

To what extent is my need for acknowledgment and attention being satisfied? This isn't only about praise, but about feedback, criticism, debate, friction. Basically, it's about being seen, and being taken seriously.

Now connect the dots you've marked on the model: the bigger the "sail," the stronger the psychological tailwind you're experiencing. The smaller the sail, the less energy you have. If you take these snapshots over an extended period, this technique will unfold its full visual potential: does the sail always point in the same direction? Does it swing to and fro? Can you identify any other patterns?

As a rule of thumb, you'll experience energy loss if you ignore these three needs, whereas your energy levels get a boost when they are satisfied. Treat your psychological hunger the same way as your bodily hunger. When your blood sugar is low, you have a snack to top up your energy reserves; similarly, if you notice that you're mentally in the amber zone, or even the red zone, ask yourself: "Which of my three psychological needs is most urgent right now? And how can I satisfy it as quickly as possible?"

Almost more important, though, is not to allow your energy reserves to run out in the first place. Rather, try to get a sense of what you need in order to fill them, and how it feels for you to be psychologically "sated." In her book *Leading with Heart, Head and Hand: The 3 Principles of Humane Leadership and Effective Change*, Anke von Platen argues that when it comes to work and projects in general, our activities are usually client-focused. Moreover, companies often allow hard data such as sales figures and deadlines to dictate their activities, and too rarely prioritize soft factors like structure, stimuli and recognition – or prioritize them only when their staff are already in the red zone.

Von Platen says that we should pay attention to our and our colleagues' resources, and that we should do this when things are going well, i.e. when we're psychologically sated. What do I need in order to feel satisfied? What is going well right now, and why? Which success factors are contributing to my mood?

Knowing our own psychological needs – and understanding how to fulfill them – is key to our happiness and effectiveness.

JOURNALING: WHY YOU SHOULD KEEP A DIARY

As the adage goes, you don't see the world as it is, you see it as you are. Doesn't the world look rosy when we're in love, and pitch-black when we're miserable? We need to understand that we can't change the world – all we can do is change our attitude toward it (see *The Circle of Influence*, p. 128). In an experiment conducted in the early 2000s, participants were asked to pause each evening to write down three good things in their lives. After just a few weeks, their stress levels were reduced. This technique is called "journaling." It's inspired by Hebb's rule, which states that the pathway between two neurons grows stronger if it's in constant use. (Conversely, if the pathway falls into disuse, it atrophies.) It isn't a question of blocking out anything negative, but of training our brains to pay more attention to the positives.

This is how you can put it into practice. Think about the day you've just had (if you're reading this in the morning, think about yesterday). In your notebook, write down three good things that happened. If you think you had a horrible day, when everything went wrong, think again – something will have gone well. Did you clean the kitchen? Did you have an interesting idea? Did you *not* vent your bad mood on your children or partner? Write it all down.

It may seem pointless, but it is a small thing you can do right now that will change your attitude to yourself and the rest of the world in the long run.

Things I did well today:

① _____

_____

② _____

_____

③ _____

_____

Write them down every evening for four weeks.

THE LAW OF REVERSED EFFORT: WHAT TO DO IF YOUR GOAL GETS IN THE WAY

In his book *The Wisdom of Insecurity*, the religious philosopher Alan Watts (1915–73) defined the "law of reversed effort" as follows:

When you try to stay on the surface of the water, you sink; but when you try to sink, you float.

To achieve your goal, you should sometimes do the opposite of what you *think* you should do. As Mark Manson says in *The Subtle Art of Not Giving a F*ck*, this law applies to all aspects of life. The more important our looks are to us, the uglier we feel, whatever we actually look like. The more important money is to us, the poorer we think we are, no matter how much money we have. The more desperately we want to be in a relationship, the more lonely (and unattractive) we appear. And the more we desire spiritual enlightenment, the more self-centered and superficial we are in our attempt to reach it.

This is how to apply the law yourself: of course there's nothing wrong with having a goal in your sights – on the contrary, many of the chapters in this book are about exactly that, because even if you miss the target or fall well short of it, you can still learn something along the way. You might even discover that the journey itself was the goal all along. But sometimes your goal can become an obstacle, and that's when the "law of reversed effect" comes into force.

Sometimes, all our efforts are in vain. Even worse, they can be counterproductive, like kicking out wildly when you're stuck in quicksand, and prevent us from turning our dreams into reality. This often happens when we're too dogged in our pursuit: the more desperate our efforts, the further our goal retreats into the distance.

Does this mean that you'll never reach your goal? No. It means that now may not be the right time to chase it. It may sound paradoxical coming from a book called *To Do*, but sometimes the one thing you should do is nothing. Experience has taught us that you can't find happiness – it finds you.

To return to Alan Watts: in another book, he quotes this ancient Zen aphorism:

Muddy water is best cleared by leaving it alone.

So when you find yourself unable to reach your goal, despite several attempts, it's a sign that you should let go of it and turn your attention to something else. Then, when the dust has settled – give it at least six months, even 18 – revisit your original goal. You will now be able to see more clearly whether it's still something you truly want. And if so, whether there might be another way to get it.

Think of a current goal of yours. What's keeping you from
reaching it?

SOURCES

Procrastination
Brenda Nguyen, Piers Steel and
Joseph R. Ferrari, "Procrastination's
Impact in the Workplace and the
Workplace's Impact on
Procrastination," *International
Journal of Selection and Assessment*
21:4, 2013.

Jason Wessel, Graham L. Bradley
and Michelle Hood, "A Low-Intensity,
High-Frequency Intervention to
Reduce Procrastination," *Applied
Psychology* 70:4, 2021.

The Pomodoro Technique
Masooma Memon, "The Science
Behind the Pomodoro Technique
and How It Helps Supercharge Your
Productivity," Focus Booster Blog,
2 April 2019.

Compartmentalization
The entrepreneur Benno Maggi told
us about this concept, and the
example is from Ryan Blair's "5
Steps of Compartmentalization: The
Secret Behind Successful
Entrepreneurs," *Forbes*, 26 June
2012.

Rapid Prototyping
See IDEO.org Design Kit for a useful
introduction. www.designkit.org/
methods/26

Bursty Communication
Christoph Riedl and Anita Williams
Woolley, "Teams vs. Crowds: A Field
Test of the Relative Contribution of
Incentives, Member Ability, and
Emergent Collaboration to Crowd-
Based Problem Solving
Performance," *Academy of
Management Discoveries* 3:4, 2017.

Inbox Management
Duncan Watts, "The Organizational
Spectroscope," Medium.com,
1 April 2016.

Adam Grant, "No, You Can't Ignore
Email. It's Rude," *The New York
Times*, 15 February 2019.

Kanban
With input from the *kanban* expert
Nadja Schnetzler: word-and-deed.
org/kanban-2

The 5 Whys Method
If you google this method, you'll find
numerous websites about it; we like
this short video from the Lean
Enterprise Institute: "Clarifying the
'5 Whys' Problem-Solving Method,"
19 July 2018,
www.youtube.com/
watch?v=SrlYkx41wEE

The 5-Second Rule
Mel Robbins, *The 5 Second Rule: Transform Your Life, Work, and Confidence with Everyday Courage* (Brentwood, TN: Savio Republic, 2017).

Triage
Panagiotis N. Skandalakis et al., "'To Afford the Wounded Speedy Assistance': Dominique Jean Larrey and Napoleon," *World Journal of Surgery* 30:8, 2006.

Paralysis by Analysis
Aesop's fable no. 605; see, for example, fablesofaesop.com/the-fox-and-the-cat.html

The Book of Books (Bob)
Pamela Paul, *My Life with Bob: Flawed Heroine Keeps Book of Books, Plot Ensues* (New York: Picador, 2017).

For Ebbinghaus's "forgetting curve," see www.mindtools.com/pages/article/forgetting-curve.htm

Getting a Project Done
Tim Stobierski, "What is Cost Estimation in Project Management?," Northeastern University blog, 11 November 2019, www.northeastern.edu/graduate/blog/cost-estimation-in-project-management/

Budgeting
Ben Aston, "Ultimate Guide to Project Budgets," DPM.

Batching
Jessica Kerr, "When Costs Are Nonlinear, Keep It Small," Jessitron, 18 January 2021.

The Delphi Method
Norman Dalkey and Olaf Helmer, "An Experimental Application of the Delphi Method to the Use of Experts," *Management Science* 9:3, 1963.

The To-Do List
For the Zeigarnik and Ovsiankina effects, see Oliver Weigelt and Christine J. Syrek, "Ovsiankina's Great Relief: How Supplemental Work during the Weekend May Contribute to Recovery in the Face of Unfinished Tasks," *International Journal of Environmental Research and Public Health* 14:12, 2017. For Ivy Lee, see James Clear, "The Ivy Lee Method: The Daily Routine Experts Recommend for Peak Productivity." For "scheduling," see Cal Newport, "The Time-Block Planner: A Daily Method for Deep Work in a Distracted World."

Motivation
J. W. Atkinson, "Motivational Determinants of Risk-Taking Behavior," *Psychological Review* 64:6, 1957.

Deep Work
Cal Newport, *Deep Work: Rules for Focused Success in a Distracted World* (New York: Grand Central Publishing, 2016).

Tactics Versus Strategies
Sun Tzu, *The Art of War* (London: Penguin, 2002).

"Strategy vs. Tactics: Why the Difference Matters," Farnam Street blog, August 2018, is a helpful introduction to this topic.

New Work
Peter Varhol, "To Agility and Beyond: The History – and Legacy – of Agile Development," TechBeacon, 26 August 2015.

Routines
Gretchen Rubin, *Better Than Before: Mastering the Habits of Our Everyday Lives* (London: Two Roads, 2015).

Appreciation
Yanfen You et al., "When and Why Saying 'Thank You' Is Better Than Saying 'Sorry' in Redressing Service Failures: The Role of Self-Esteem," *Journal of Marketing* 84:2, 2019.

Radical Transparency
Ray Dalio, "How to Build a Company Where the Best Ideas Win," TED, 6 September 2017.

Sandwich Feedback
Angela M. Legg and Kate Sweeny, "Do You Want the Good News or the Bad News First? The Nature and Consequences of News Order Preferences," *Personality and Social Psychology Bulletin* 40:3, 2013.

Likeability
Tiziana Casciaro and Miguel Sousa Lobo, "Competent Jerks, Lovable Fools, and the Formation of Social Networks," *Harvard Business Review*, June 2005.

The Theory of Small Gifts
Reid Hoffman, "Connections with Integrity," *Strategy+Business*, Summer 2012.

Brainstorming
Alex Osborn, *Your Creative Power: How to Use Imagination* (New York: Scribner, 1948).

Tomas Chamorro-Premuzic, "Why Group Brainstorming Is a Waste of Time," *Harvard Business Review*, 25 March 2015.

Vicky L. Putman and Paul Paulus, "Brainstorming, Brainstorming Rules and Decision Making," *Journal of Creative Behavior* 43:1, 2009.

Structured Evaluation
Our own creation, with input from the ideas expert Markus Mettler. See www.brainstore.com

The Circle of Competence
Warren Buffett, "Chairman's Letter," Berkshire Hathaway Inc, 1996. Berkshire Hathaway Inc., Annual Meeting (afternoon session), 3 May 1999, CNBC Warren Buffett Archive (at 33'42").

The 5/25 Rule
The Art of Improvement, "Warren Buffett's 5/25 Rule Will Help You Focus on the Things That Matter," 2 September 2018, www.youtube.com/watch?v=gkhtYs22bLI.

The idea wasn't Warren Buffett's: see Ruth Umoh, "The Surprising Lesson This 25-Year-Old Learned from Asking Warren Buffett an Embarrassing Question," CNBC, 2 September 2019.

The Circle of Influence
Stephen R. Covey, *The 7 Habits of Highly Effective People: Powerful Lessons in Personal Change*, revised and updated edn (New York: Simon & Schuster, 2020).

Disruptive Innovation
Clayton M. Christensen, *The Innovator's Dilemma: When New Technologies Cause Great Firms to Fail* (Boston: Harvard Business Review Press, 1997).

Kotter's 8-Step Model of Change
John P. Kotter, *Leading Change* (Boston: Harvard Business Review Press, 2012).

A New Map of Life
For the Stanford Center on Longevity, see longevity.stanford.edu/a-new-map-of-life/

Project Evaluation
The entrepreneur Benno Maggi introduced us to the concept, and we tweaked and expanded it.

The Myth of Achievement
Steffen Hillmert, "Meritokratie als Mythos, Maßstab und Motor gesellschaftlicher Ungleichheit" ("Meritocracy as Myth, Yardstick and Driver of Social Inequality"), lecture given at the Second Regional Conference of the German Society for Sociology, Jena, September 2019.

The Matthew Effect
Robert K. Merton, "The Matthew Effect in Science," *Science* 159:3810, 1968.

The Transactional Model
Anke von Platen, *Führen mit Herz, Kopf und Hand: Die 3 Prinzipien für menschliche Führung und erfolgreiche Veränderungen* (Leading with Heart, Head and Hand: The 3 Principles of Humane Leadership and Effective Change) (Norderstedt: Books on Demand, 2018).

Journaling
Karen A. Baikie and Kay Wilhelm, "Emotional and Physical Health Benefits of Expressive Writing," *Advances in Psychiatric Treatment* 11:5, 2005.

The Law of Reversed Effort
Alan Watts, *The Wisdom of Insecurity: A Message for an Age of Anxiety* (London: Rider, 2021).
Alan Watts, *The Way of Zen* (London: Ebury, 2021).

Mark Manson, *The Subtle Art of Not Giving a F*ck: A Counterintuitive Approach to Living a Good Life* (San Francisco: HarperOne, 2016).

ABOUT THE AUTHORS

Mikael Krogerus, born in Stockholm, is an editor at *Das Magazin* in Zurich. He has previously worked for *Der Freitag* and the *Neue Zürcher Zeitung*'s *Folio* supplement, among others.

Roman Tschäppeler, born in Bern, founded the guzo.ch studio in 2003, where he produces films and advertising campaigns, and helps companies develop their ideas.

They are both alumni of the Kaospilot business school in Denmark, and the authors of, among others, the international bestseller *The Decision Book: Fifty Models for Strategic Thinking*. Their books have been translated into more than 25 languages and have sold millions of copies.

www.rtmk.ch

ACKNOWLEDGMENTS

It takes a village to raise a child – and two villages to write a book. We are deeply grateful to the following people for their help in creating this book:

Simon Brunner, Teresa Bücker, Finn Canonica, Daniel Crewe, Louisa Dunnigan, Phil Earnhart, Maurice Ettlin, Frances Frei, Christof Gertsch, Ulrike Groeger, Dag Grødal, Peter Haag, J. D. Kemming, Anne-Laure Le Cunff, Benno Maggi, Ondine Riesen, Franziska Schutzbach, Roger Tinner, Johanna von Rauch, Sven Weber, Andreas Wellnitz and Hanna Nilsson Zettersten.

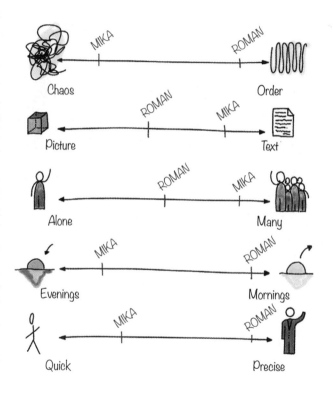